Oceanic
and Australasian
Mythology

LIBRARY OF THE WORLD'S
MYTHS AND LEGENDS

Oceanic
and Australasian
Mythology

Roslyn Poignant

NEWNES BOOKS

Half-title page. A turtle-shell mask worn in the Bomai–Malu cult ceremonies of the Torres Straits. Pitt Rivers Museum, Oxford.

Frontispiece. Ngwalndu or clan spirits of the Abelam in a Maprik ceremonial house, Sepik, Papua New Guinea.

Oceanic Mythology first published 1967.
New revised edition, *Oceanic and Australasian Mythology,* published 1985 by Newnes Books,
a division of The Hamlyn Publishing Group Limited,
84–88 The Centre, Feltham, Middlesex, TW13 4BH,
and distributed for them by
Hamlyn Distribution Services,
Rushden, Northants, England.

ISBN 0 600 34283 2

Printed in Yugoslavia

Contents

Introduction

Australasia encompasses the world's second largest island, New Guinea, and its smallest continent, Australia, together with New Zealand and adjacent islands. Beyond to the north and east lie the multitude of small islands of Oceania scattered like beads from a broken necklace across the wide Pacific. The three regions of Oceania are the western or inner ring of Melanesian archipelagoes and islands; the small islands of Micronesia in the northwest Pacific; and the Polynesian islands which lie within a great triangle extending from the Hawaiian Islands in the north to Easter Island 2486 miles (4000 kilometres) from the South American coast, and south to New Zealand in temperate seas. The cultural, physical and linguistic characteristics of these regions shade one into another in such a way as to suggest a complex history of migration and settlement of the whole area. (See map, pp. 20–21).

Today it is only in parts of New Guinea and in the isolated islands of central Micronesia, where there has been relatively unbroken continuity with the past, that traditional beliefs expressed in mythic form continue to provide the main cohesive force in the society. On the other hand, the New Guineans, the Pacific Islanders, the Maoris, and the original Australians are today reclaiming their traditional heritage. In the words of the Australian Aboriginal poet Kath Walker, they are asking: 'Why change our sacred myths for your sacred myths?'

In the past two decades since the first edition of this book was published a number of Pacific peoples have gained or are gaining political, if not economic, independence. (See

p. 21). Others, like the Maoris and the Australian Aborigines, are trying to assert their separate identities within white-dominated societies. In the struggle old mythologies and associated rituals have been reanimated and new cultural identities are being forged out of the old traditions. Fundamental to these movements has been the issue of Land Rights: access to it, control over its resources, sovereignty over it, or compensation for being isolated from it. The Australian Aborigines' Land Rights claims, and the Nauruan and Banaban Islanders' battles for compensation from the

Chimbu tribesmen dance before setting out for a neighbouring pig-kill, Central Highlands of New Guinea.

phosphate companies may be couched in the language of Western economics, but it is our failure to understand their broader concept of land that has forced them to bargain in our terminology. For them land has not only an economic value which may range from the provision of subsistence to income from the lease of mining rights, but it is also imbued with spiritual essence. In 1980 when Jim Bienderry, the Aboriginal elder from Noonkanbah, Western Australia, presented his case to the United Nations sub-committee on Minority Rights at Geneva against drilling on land sacred to the Great Goanna Spirit, he was using the language of myth to express an Aboriginal relationship with nature. The intricacies of this worldview will be explored in a later section (p. 114).

Pacific Islands have sometimes been likened to laboratory situations, mainly because it is possible to observe the effects of isolation on founder groups of similar stock settled in very different environments. But in the late 20th century this analogy takes on a fresh significance. The atom-bomb-blasted Bikini atoll and the barren moonscape of Banaba

(Ocean Island), mined of phosphates down to the coral core, provide two fearful examples of man-made ecological disaster. In spite, however, of the devastation of their lands both groups of islanders have retained a strong sense of their cultural identities. The Bikinians have tried several times to resettle their atoll, but recently it has been declared uninhabitable for at least another 30 years. Similarly only a token number of Banabans live on their home island. Since 1946 the majority have lived in exile on Rambi island which they purchased from Fiji with phosphate royalties, and they have become citizens of Fiji. Their own land, Banaba, is now part of newly independent Kiribati. Although the Banabans draw much of their spiritual strength from their strong Christian faith their attachment to their land is deeply rooted in traditional spiritual beliefs. It is an attitude which by its affirmation of the interdependence of humankind and nature provides a more positive model for a strategy of global survival.

The Lands

What were these lands of the original Australians and Pacific Islanders? The most well-known feature of the Australian continent is the uniqueness of its flora and fauna, evolved during the millenia of its isolation. Although it is a remarkably uniform land-form, in that less than one-tenth of its surface rises above 656 yards (600 metres), it is distinguished by a variety of habitats, including the humid subtropical north, fertile eastern coasts, cool southern mountains, and dry deserts of the interior. To the north of it equatorial New Guinea also exhibits environmental extremes ranging from dry rain-shadow areas and steamy swamps to cooler highlands where, in Irian Jaya, snow stays on the peaks.

Vastly different are the island worlds cradled by the Pacific. This great ocean, which occupies more than a third of the earth's surface, both unites and separates them. Its

tides, currents and winds influence their structure, climate and vegetation and carried humankind to almost every scrap of habitable land. The equitable climate and good living provided by some islands caused their first European visitors to dub them paradises, but many support only a precarious existence. In the zone west of a line which runs south from Japan along the line of the Marianas and east of the Carolines, then dips south in a wide arc east of Fiji, Tonga and New Zealand are found larger, relatively fertile continental islands, formed from the rocks of the Australasian shelf. East of this line is the true Pacific Basin where the much smaller islands are of three main kinds: high or volcanic islands, raised coral islands and low islands or coral atolls. Volcanic islands of basaltic rock upthrust from the ocean floor are usually surrounded by fringing reefs and tend to have better climates and support wider ranges of vegetation, thus providing for more diversified ways of life. Those which lie in the path of trade winds have wet windward sides and dry leeward sides. Raised coral islands have been formed out of successive elevations of ancient coral reefs, and some like Nauru have rich deposits of guano. Many coral atolls did not exist until late Pleistocene times when lowered sea levels exposed coral reefs and provided the conditions for atoll formation; this process involved the subsidence of a central volcanic island, leaving a lagoon enclosed by old reefs on which land had built up. The soils of coral atolls are thin, water is scarce, and they are vulnerable to drought and the destructive force of tropical storms and typhoons. Nevertheless the richness of marine life sheltered by their fringing reefs enables some to support

Above Prehistoric stone image, Chimbu district, Central Highlands of New Guinea. There are several types of stone carving, found in many parts of New Guinea, which, although they have not been made by the present inhabitants, exhibit continuities in style with more recent carvings. As found objects, however, their owners regard them as stones of power – bringing success with gardens, pigs, children, friends and – in the old days – fighting.

Top Lime spatula from the Trobriand Islands. Pitt Rivers Museum, Oxford.

Opposite The carved wall panel in the Maori meeting house, Te Hono Ki Rarotonga, at Tokomaru Bay, North Island, New Zealand, built in the 1920s, represents a mythological sea creature, the *marakihau,* with syphon tongue.

amazingly high populations. The utilisation of their potential resources, however, required founding groups who were already skilled horticulturists and fishermen.

Many Pacific Islands form clusters or are part of island complexes, while others stand alone – and each type of island grouping provides a different kind of ecosystem which, in turn, allows for a different set of cultural options. Whatever the grouping there is a critical population limit after which various social mechanisms such as infanticide, abortion, famine, warfare, and migration help to maintain it. Kapingarangi, a Polynesian outlier 367 miles (590 kilometres)

the mechanism for access to the resources was provided by an intricate system of tribute and gift exchange according to a ranking system controlled by the paramount district of Gagil on Yap. (See p. 75).

The Discoverers

The story of the discovery of these vast and diverse regions of Australasia and Oceania is one of the great chapters in humankind's prehistory. It begins 70,000 to 50,000 years ago when sea levels were much lower than they are today and land-forms were different. Island and mainland Southeast Asia formed a geographical entity, Sundaland, and east of it – across a deep sea barrier – lay the land-mass of Greater Australia which then comprised Australia and New Guinea. The warm and shallow seas of Sundaland provided just the right conditions for the Australoid hunter-gatherers who lived there to learn to exploit the marine life and to master the simple watercraft that enabled them to make the passage through island-studded seas to Greater Australia; thus these people were amongst the first sea voyagers in the world.

The size and number of these founder groups, and the routes they took remain matters for speculation, partly because many early coastal settlement sites are now submerged. But 40,000 years ago these first Australians were already camped on the banks of the Swan River, Western Australia. Settlement sites of similar antiquity have been found in southeastern Australia. It is argued that the pursuit of big game in the shape of giant marsupials would have provided the impetus for a rapid spread across the continent, but it is more probable that the process of adaptation to the variety of habitats encountered could have taken 10,000 to 20,000 years. By some 25,000 years ago, after the land bridge between mainland Australia and Tasmania had formed, all parts of Greater Australia, including what is now New Guinea, were inhabited,

north of Melanesian New Ireland, is only a half square mile (1.3 square kilometres) and 10 feet (3 metres) above sea level. Although it is one of the smallest inhabited atolls it supports a stable community. Easter Island is a high island isolate; its sheer cliffs face southern seas and its nearest neighbour is Pitcairn Island 1491 miles (2400 kilometres) to the west. By the time of European contact its resources were apparently overtaxed, mainly because of deafforestation, and warfare and violence were rife. Ten degrees south of the equator two tiny atolls, Manihiki and Rakahanga form an island cluster. Separated by only 25 miles (40 kilometres)

of ocean, the traditional pattern of living in pre-contact times was for the inhabitants to spend some time on each island in turn, thus allowing the vegetation on the deserted island to recover and the lagoon to be restocked. Long distance inter-island voyaging is necessary to take advantage of the enlarged ecosystems provided by island complexes, and this required canoe-building, sailing and navigational skills of a high order. Island complexes may be chains of islands as in the Marshalls, or they may include one or more volcanic islands. For example the central and western Caroline Islands form a complex centred on Yap, and

except perhaps for the central deserts and the cool southern mountains. Over the following thousands of years climatic changes, induced by fluctuating sea levels, combined with changes wrought by the inhabitants themselves – particularly by their use of fire to manage the land – changed patterns of subsistence and hastened the extinction of some of the giant marsupials. Some 16,000 years ago seas began to rise again, gradually flooding the great northern plains of Arafura and Carpentaria, increasing the distance between Australia and New Guinea until, by 6000 years ago, the last narrow land bridge was cut. Thereafter their prehistorics diverged more sharply. Although the wild dog, the dingo, did not arrive in Australia for probably another thousand years it spread rapidly throughout the continent – except for Tasmania which had again been separated from the mainland by the sea 6000 years earlier. Separated by longer seaways, Australia's first inhabitants remained primarily hunter-gatherers.

The rising seas had also submerged ancient Sundaland creating island Southeast Asia, thus providing some of the impetus for a new movement eastwards of a neolithic people who were horticulturists and fishermen. The bold seafarers of this great expansion were Austronesian language speakers of Mongoloid stock from whom both the Micronesians and the Polynesians are descended. A reconstruction of the ancestral or proto-Austronesian language shows they cultivated the banana, coconut, breadfruit, taro, yams, aroids, sugar cane and sago; domesticated the dog, pig and fowl; made tools of ground stone, wood and shell; possessed a range of fishing techniques; and made pots. Their spiritual beliefs included ancestor worship, nature deities and local spirits and the concept of *tapu*. They were explorers and colonisers and their outrigger sailing canoes provided the essential transport for their cultural baggage. Their need for canoe captains and craft specialists suggests that they may already have possessed a ranked social structure.

When the Austronesians reached New Guinea about 3000 B.C. and pushed on into the Melanesian archipelagoes they encountered the Papuans who were derived from Australoid stock and – in some places – Negrito groups. In the New Guinea highlands some of these early settlers had been using techniques of drainage and irrigation to cultivate a crop – probably taro – for at least a thousand years, and it seems possible that this was an independent development of the techniques of plant cultivation. The Papuans were well established and the Austronesians only gained a foothold along the northern and southeastern coast of New Guinea. However, the complex exchange of genes, languages and cultural traits which took place between the two groups contributed to the physical, linguistic and cultural diversity that characterises Melanesia today.

The distinguishing artefact of these Austronesians was their style of decorated pottery called Lapita. The archaeological record shows that by 1300 B.C. it had spread through the Melanesian archipelagoes to Fiji, Tonga and Samoa. Supported by the linguistic evidence of a proto-Polynesian language it is evident that these central Pacific islands were the cradle of a Polynesian people and culture, but a thousand more years of cultural consolidation took place before their descendents set out from Samoa across unknown seas to eastern Polynesia. The possibility of another northern migration route via Micronesia into western Polynesia cannot be ruled out entirely. By 1500 B.C. Belau and the Marianas in western Micronesia had also been settled by Austronesian speakers directly from Indonesia and the Philippines, but in eastern Micronesia the major migration was from the robust Lapita culture area to the south, and Kiribati, the Marshall Islands and east Caroline Islands were settled in the first millenium A.D.

On present archaeological evidence the scenario for the settlement of eastern and marginal Polynesia gives a Marquesan site primacy, but both the Marquesan and Society Islands

Above Carved wooden ancestor figure, Easter Island. Museum of Mankind, London.

Opposite A lagoon fringed by coral reefs, Ra'iatea, French Polynesia, in the eastern Pacific.

had probably been reached by the first century A.D. Thereafter both groups were dispersal centres for the settlement of the rest of eastern and marginal Polynesia. By A.D. 500 Easter Island had been reached, probably from the Marquesas, and the Hawaiian Islands may well have been settled by founder groups from both centres. The ancestors of the Maoris did not reach New Zealand until A.D. 1000.

Recent computer analysis of 100,000 conjectured inter-island voyages has demonstrated, firstly, that it would have been impossible for the Polynesians to have made any of their great discoveries by drift voyaging. To reach some of their destinations they must have sailed into the wind by as much as 90 degrees. That the Polynesians – and the Micronesians – possessed the necessary navigational and sailing techniques is no longer doubted. Secondly, the highest number of settlement-by-drift possibilities occur east-west in the central Pacific and these could have accounted for the 'back migrations' to Polynesian

outliers in Melanesia. It has also been established that two-way inter-island voyaging habitually took place within a number of different 'contact zones', and the voyage in the 1970s of the double canoe, *Hokule'a,* from Hawaii to Tahiti and back with a Micronesian navigator, has also demonstrated the feasibility of long distance two-way voyaging. Many of the reasons for the outward thrust from eastern Polynesia – famine, defeat in war, affairs of passion, theft, and the questing spirit of the Polynesians – are recounted in their myths. Whatever the reasons, after each canoe party had settled on a new island, the developing community evolved its own unique way of life in an isolation that sometimes lasted for centuries or was occasionally broken by chance voyagers blown off course, or by deliberate colonisers seeking a new home.

The European Invasion

When the world's first circumnavigator, Magellan, sailed across the

Pacific and reached Guam in 1521 his men killed many of the inhabitants and burnt their houses and canoes in retaliation for the theft of a skiff. This clash heralded a European invasion of the Pacific which was to attain its full impact in the 19th century. The men who followed the explorers came for what they could take. They came for the sandalwood, the pearlshell, the whales and the men and women. Labour was wanted for copra production, and for the sugar plantations of Queensland, Fiji and Hawaii. When the local inhabitants were unwilling to work, Asiatic labour was introduced. In the 1860s about 1000 Easter Islanders were press-ganged to work the guano deposits of Chile. The hundred odd who survived to be repatriated were reduced to fifteen by an epidemic of smallpox. This last remnant carried the disease to the island, and the attendant famine and strife further reduced the population to 600. By 1868 the chiefs and priests were dead and this broken and hostile people had been converted to Christianity. The newcomers to the area also

wanted land and to get it they plundered, killed, introduced disease, stirred up warring factions against each other and supplied the lethal gun. No condensed account can convey the drastic changes wrought in the physical and spiritual life of the indigenous peoples during this period. In the vastness of Australia the relentless dispossession of the Aborigines almost passed unnoticed, but in Tasmania it was concentrated in the Black Drive of 1830 from which only a handful survived.

In all this horror perhaps only the missionaries acted with any humanity or held out any hope of social stability, but they too wanted something – they wanted souls. In many island communities the acceptance of the powerful god of the newcomers was accompanied by the total and deliberate destruction of their own gods. The Rev. W. Ellis described in *Polynesian Researches* how the Tahitians burned their gods, small carved wooden images or shapeless logs of wood covered with sennit braid and feather decoration. In Hapaai of the Tongan group the missionary John Williams watched while the gods were hung from 'the rafters of the house in which they had been adored'. Williams cut one down, and with the cord still round its neck, shipped it back to England.

This turbulent colonial history has influenced the shape of the emergent nations. They include relatively homogeneous single island states like prosperous Nauru which is only 9 miles square (24 kilometres square), Papua New Guinea which comprises a multiplicity of tribes, and Fiji where the Fijians are outnumbered by the descendants of the Indian indentured labourers who first arrived in 1879. In many places depopulation of the outer islands has taken place as the people have been attracted to the growing urban centres. For instance, two-thirds of the 160,000 French Polynesians of the five archipelagoes now live in Tahiti and over half of these are concentrated in Papeete urban zone. Tourism and the infrastructure set up for the French nuclear tests provide the support system. But increased urbanisation throughout the Pacific has meant increased separation of the people from their ancestral lands and has reduced the majority to the status of wage labourers, subject to the usual urban ills. In many islands overpopulation has provided the impetus for emigration. There are 60,000 Samoans on U.S.A.'s west coast – twice as many as in Samoa – and 20,000 more are in Hawaii. Similarly there are about as many Wallis Islanders in New Caledonia as there are in the home islands, so that together with the Europeans, the Vietnamese and others they outnumber the New Caledonians. Within Micronesia Guam probably acts as the greatest magnet for migrants, but the tiny islet of Ibeye, with a population of 4000, is a dormitory town for the workers on the U.S. missile testing grounds of Kwajaleen atoll, Marshall Islands. Not only have the Polynesian Pukapukans migrated to Rarotonga and New Zealand, they have also purchased an island, Nassau, from New Zealand for their surplus population.

Socio-political changes of this magnitude have loosened traditional bonds and the creative energies released have flowed into new art-forms and written literature, both in the vernacular and in the languages of the colonial powers. But the traditional performance arts of song, dance, and ceremony, involving masks, costumes and other ceremonial paraphernalia have also been revitalised. Innovative use has been made of new materials and traditional decorative motifs have been incorporated in new symbolic structures such as the contemporary Maori meeting house, or the modern Sepik council houses in New Guinea. In Australia there are Aboriginal Arts Boards, Cultural Foundations, and local oral literature centres where myths and legends can be tape-recorded. New Guinea now has a university, National Museum and National Art School which provide pan-tribal loci for the development of a national identity. Additionally a number of regional centres, notably the Gogodala Centre on the Papuan

Gulf, have seen remarkable community-based revivals of traditional arts, crafts and ceremonies. Similarly the University of the South Pacific in Suva is a pan-Pacific institution which holds art workshops in Kiribati, the Solomons, Vanuatu, Samoa, Tonga, Rarotonga and Fiji. South Pacific Arts Festivals provide the occasions for cultural syncretism, and various symposia on Oceanic Arts and Culture (in which the participant-specialists are often indigenous people) provide a forum for discussion of such burning issues as the return of important cultural objects, and other aspects of cultural colonialism, for example, the role of tourism which provides patronage for a revival of the traditional performance arts – and an income for the performers – while at the same time it commercialises and trivialises them. Although the myths of the original Australians and the Pacific Islanders – like song and dance – often survive only as entertainment, even in this role they retain a cohesive function and may reflect a deep profundity.

The Myths

If we are to recover even fragments of those mythical truths which inspired the Pacific cultures which were shattered by the coming of the European, we must turn to the early accounts of explorers, travellers, missionaries, traders, and colonial administrators, for although they were the instruments of change they were also the great recorders of Oceanic lore.

Joseph Banks, Captain Cook's companion of the first voyage, was perhaps the first European to attempt an account of the customs, traditions, beliefs and material culture of an island society, Tahiti. His tantalisingly brief comments are often the only information which has survived about certain traditions. For instance, both Cook and Banks saw an enormous figure of the great Polynesian hero, Maui, which had strange knob-like protuberances that the Tahitians called 'little men'. They were told it

was a puppet, but Banks regretted his inability to understand more detailed explanations and Cook wrote that the tales he was told about Maui were too absurd to repeat. How we long to know more.

In 1797 The London Missionary Society's ship the *Duff* arrived in the Society Islands. It was the missionaries' determination to spread the *true* Gospel which led them to learn the languages and compile dictionaries, and in the process record the traditions of the people. One of the earliest of these was the Rev. W. Ellis who, although he too thought the Polynesian stories absurd and sometimes indecent, could not help observing that 'By their rude mythology, their lovely islands were made a sort of fairyland. . . . The mountain's summit, and the fleecy mists that hang upon its brows – the rocky defile – the foamy cataract – and the lonely dell – were all regarded as the abode of invisible beings.'

When, in 1845, Sir George Grey was 'suddenly and unexpectedly' appointed Governor of New Zealand at a time when the discontent of the Maoris had developed into open hostility, his realisation that myth had an important function led him to compile the first collection of *Polynesian Mythology*, published first in

Above The engraving depicts the occasion when the Rarotongans, in the fervour of their conversion to Christianity, brought fourteen of their staff gods to the missionaries. Some were torn to pieces before their eyes, others were reserved for the rafters of the chapel and some were brought back to Europe. (*See* page 38.) Title page illustration of *A Narrative of Missionary Enterprise in the South Seas,* by John Williams.

Top Initiation ceremony for chief Poulaho's son, Tonga. Engraving after J. Webber's drawing made on Cook's third voyage.

Opposite In 1868 the stone figure called 'Breaking Waves' was removed from a stone house in the sacred village of Orongo, Easter Island. The village was only inhabited at the time of the election of the bird man, and the statue was in some way associated with the cult. Museum of Mankind, London.

Maori, and then in English in 1855. 'To my surprise', he wrote, 'I found that these chiefs ... frequently quoted, in explanation of their views and intentions, fragments of ancient poems or proverbs, or made allusions which rested on an ancient system of mythology; and, although it was clear that the most important parts of their communications were embodied in these figurative forms, the interpreters were quite at fault, they could rarely (if ever) translate the poems or explain the allusions. . . . I should add that even the great majority of young Christian Maoris were quite as much at fault on these subjects as were the European interpreters.'

So for eight years he spent his time learning the language and persuading the priests to teach him the esoteric lore. He came to realise that these myths had many variants, known all over New Zealand. Moreover, many of these Maori themes and motifs were shared with the rest of Polynesia.

Grey's book certainly quickened romantic interest in the Pacific but it also attracted the attention of early ethnologists like E. B. Tylor. His name heads the list of illustrious scholars – Max Müller, Frobenius, Adolf Bastian, Sir James Frazer, Sigmund Freud – who in the years that

followed, sought to use the myths of Oceania to support their theories concerning mythology, culture and society.

Grey's footsteps were also followed by the many dedicated amateur ethnologists of the 19th century whose various occupations brought them into touch with the indigenous people; and one cannot overestimate the importance of their contribution. To name only a few: by 1850, J. M. Orsmond, preacher, schoolmaster and chief of native police, had made a definitive collection of texts, chants and myths from Tahiti and the neighbouring islands. His manuscript was lost in the Paris archives but eighty years later his granddaughter Teuira Henry produced *Ancient Tahiti*, a reconstruction from his original notes. The indefatigable recorder of *Hawaiian Antiquities and Folklore* was Abraham Fornander, a circuit judge and inspector of schools. In Australia, F. J. Gillan, magistrate and Protector of Aborigines of Alice Springs, collaborated with Sir Baldwin Spencer in his studies of the Aranda and other Central and Northern Australian tribes.

With the arrival of the Europeans the Polynesians also rediscovered themselves. Tupaia, a Tahitian priest, sailed with Cook to New Zealand

and found that the Maoris still spoke of their homeland to the north, although there had been no contact for centuries. He was followed by many other Polynesian travellers who certainly took their songs and stories with them. Perhaps the stories of the Polynesian hero Maui, which are known in Melanesian New Hebrides, only reached there with Simeona, a Polynesian missionary in 1859. The Polynesians also quickly learnt to read and write and from mid-century on they began to record their own traditions. Some Hawaiians, mostly the students of the Rev. Dibble's Lahainaluna School, began to publish, in their own language newspapers, the many romantic narratives for which the activities of their gods and heroes served as models. More important still King Kalakaua wrote down the Kumulipo Birth Chant of Creation, a genealogical record of his ancestors. He did this at the instigation of Adolf Bastian who recognised its importance.

In New Zealand the Maoris' awareness of what was happening to their people as a result of the passing of the old ways culminated in an attempt to record their vanishing knowledge. In the 1850s a group of east coast Maoris chose a *tohunga* or priest, Te Matarohanga, to lecture them on the ancient lore, as he had done in the past in the *Whare Wananga*, or schools of sacred learning. What he had to say was written down by two 'scribes'. Years later it was translated by S. Percy Smith and published as *The Lore of the Whare Wananga*. Nothing could express more strongly than Te Matarohanga's own words the binding function of myths in the social order and his awareness of the irrevocable nature of its passing. He told his listeners to 'Be very careful in reciting these valuable teachings that your ancestors have collected during the past generations right away from the period of Rangi, the Sky Father and Papa, the Earth Mother, down to the present day; even though the teachings from the Whare Wananga are mere shreds....' He gave as the reason for this disintegration men's failure to perform the rituals and their loss of faith in the gods. This meant, he said, that they could no longer acquire the *mana* (power) to use this ancient knowledge. He concluded: 'I say also to you that those things you are writing from my dictation are but the ends, fragments of the truths, a portion of sacred things, for the anciently established true teaching has become effaced....'

There are as many valid versions of a myth as there are story-tellers to recount it, and very often the interest lies in the difference between several versions. I have therefore tried to avoid, with a few exceptions, giving a composite version of a myth. The following stories have been selected from those collected by the explorers, travellers, missionaries, government officials, anthropologists and other scholars who have recorded and commented on the oral literature and traditions of the people of the Pacific. The source of those discussed at any length is given in the text.

Above The Maori meeting house embodies the traditional history and spiritual values of the tribe. To Kanganui a Noho at Te Kuiti was a gift to the Maniapoto tribe from the guerrilla leader Te Kooti for the protection afforded himself and his followers in 1872–83. The subjects of its panel carvings are inter-tribal and include Maui, the demi-god, Kupe, traditionally regarded as the discoverer of New Zealand, and the founder ancestor of the Arawa tribe, Tama te Kapua. More recent ancestors are represented in photographs.

Top Traditional designs and themes have been used to decorate Ambunti district council house, on the Sepik river, Papua New Guinea.

Opposite William Hodges painted this impressive record of the fleet of war canoes at Tahiti on Cook's second voyage. There were 160 double canoes, each with its own fighting stage, and as many small canoes. This painting is one of the few records of canoe figureheads of gods or guardian spirits set one on top of the other. National Maritime Museum, London.

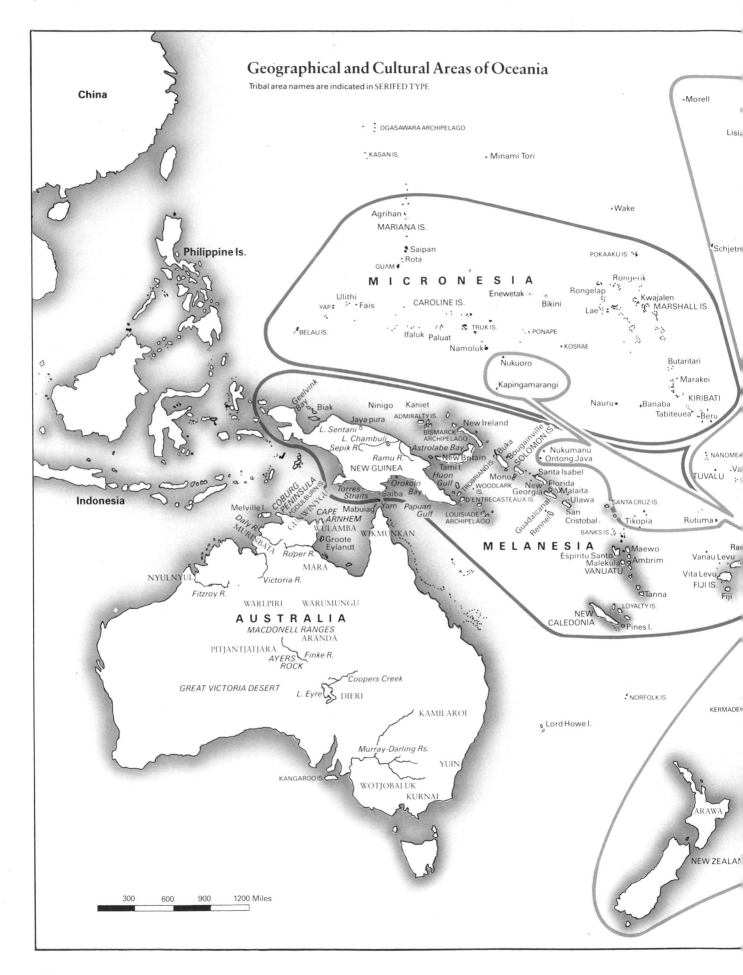

Geographical and Cultural Areas of Oceania

Tribal area names are indicated in SERIFED TYPE

China

• Morell

Lisia

OGASAWARA ARCHIPELAGO

KASAN IS.

• Minami Tori

• Wake

Agrihan
MARIANA IS.

Schjetn

Philippine Is.

POKAAKU IS.

• Saipan
• Rota
GUAM

MICRONESIA

Rongerik
Rongelap
Enewetak   Bikini   Lae   Kwajalen
MARSHALL IS.

Ulithi
YAP   Fais   CAROLINE IS.

BELAU IS.
Ifaluk   Paluat   TRUK IS.

PONAPE

• KOSRAE

Namoluk

Butaritari

Nukuoro

Marakei

Kapingamarangi

Nauru
Banaba   KIRIBATI
Tabiteuea   Beru

Indonesia

Geelvink
Bay   Biak
Jaya pura
L. Sentani
L. Chambuli
Sepik R.
Ramu R.

Ninigo   Kaniet
ADMIRALTY IS.

New Ireland
BISMARCK
ARCHIPELAGO
Astrolabe Bay

Buka
Bougainville
SOLOMON IS.

NANOMEA
Va

NEW GUINEA   New Britain
Tami I.
Huon
Gulf

Nukumanu
Ontong Java

TUVALU

Melville I.
COBURG
PENINSULA
Torres   GUNWINYGU
Straits   Saiba
CAPE   Mabuiag   Yam
ARNHEM   Papuan
WULAMBA   Gulf
MURINBATA   Groote
Eylandt
Roper R.

Orokolo
Bay
TROBRIAND IS.
WOODLARK
IS.
Mono
New
Georgia
D'ENTRECASTEAUX IS.

Santa Isabel
Florida
Malaita
Ulawa
San
Cristobal
Rennell

SANTA CRUZ IS.
Tikopia

Rotuma

NYULNYUL
Daly R.

LOUISIADE
ARCHIPELAGO
Guadalcanal

BANKS IS.

Ra
Vanau Levu

Vita Levu
FIJI IS.
Fiji

MARA
Victoria R.

WIKMUNKAN

MELANESIA

Espiritu Santo
Malekula
VANUATU

Maewo
Ambrim

Tanna

WARLPIRI   WARUMUNGU

AUSTRALIA

MACDONELL RANGES
ARANDA

PITJANTJATJARA
AYERS
ROCK   Finke R.

GREAT VICTORIA DESERT
L. Eyre   DIERI

Coopers Creek

NEW
CALEDONIA   Pines I.

LOYALTY IS.

NORFOLK IS.

Lord Howe I.

KERMADE

KAMILAROI

Murray-Darling Rs.

YUIN

KANGAROO IS.
WOTJOBALUK
KURNAI

ARAWA

NEW ZEALAN

300   600   900   1200 Miles

20

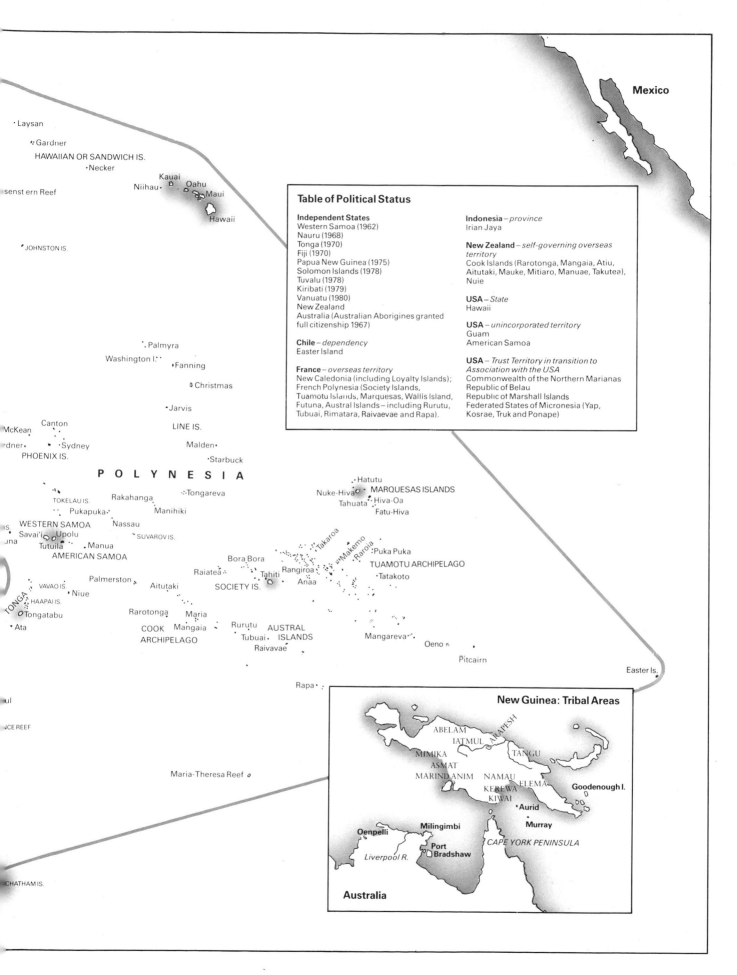

Mexico

· Laysan

·: Gardner

HAWAIIAN OR SANDWICH IS.

·Necker

senst ern Reef

Kauai
Niihau· Oahu
Maui

Hawaii

· JOHNSTON IS.

Table of Political Status

Independent States
Western Samoa (1962)
Nauru (1968)
Tonga (1970)
Fiji (1970)
Papua New Guinea (1975)
Solomon Islands (1978)
Tuvalu (1978)
Kiribati (1979)
Vanuatu (1980)
New Zealand
Australia (Australian Aborigines granted
full citizenship 1967)

Chile – *dependency*
Easter Island

France – *overseas territory*
New Caledonia (including Loyalty Islands);
French Polynesia (Society Islands,
Tuamotu Islands, Marquesas, Wallis Island,
Futuna, Austral Islands – including Rurutu,
Tubuai, Rimatara, Raivaevae and Rapa).

Indonesia – *province*
Irian Jaya

New Zealand – *self-governing overseas
territory*
Cook Islands (Rarotonga, Mangaia, Atiu,
Aitutaki, Mauke, Mitiaro, Manuae, Takutea),
Nuie

USA – *State*
Hawaii

USA – *unincorporated territory*
Guam
American Samoa

USA – *Trust Territory in transition to
Association with the USA*
Commonwealth of the Northern Marianas
Republic of Belau
Republic of Marshall Islands
Federated States of Micronesia (Yap,
Kosrae, Truk and Ponape)

· Palmyra

Washington I.·· ·Fanning

0 Christmas

· Jarvis

Canton
McKean
LINE IS.
rdner· ·Sydney Malden·
PHOENIX IS.
·Starbuck

P O L Y N E S I A

·Hatutu
·:Tongareva Nuke-Hiva○ · MARQUESAS ISLANDS
Rakahanga Tahuata ·· ·Hiva-Oa
TOKELAU IS. ·. Fatu-Hiva
Pukapuka Manihiki
WESTERN SAMOA Nassau
S. · Savai'i Upolu ~ SUVAROV IS.
una Tutuila ·Manua
AMERICAN SAMOA

·Takaroa
·Makemo
Bora Bora ·Raroia Puka Puka
Raiatea· Rangiroa TUAMOTU ARCHIPELAGO
Palmerston· Tahiti ·Tatakoto
VAVAO IS. Aitutaki SOCIETY IS. Anaa
TONGA ·Niue
HAAPAI IS. Rarotonga Maria
○Tongatabu Mangaia ·Rurutu AUSTRAL
· Ata COOK Tubuai· ISLANDS Mangareva·· ·
ARCHIPELAGO Raivavae · Oeno ·
·
Pitcairn
Easter Is.
ul Rapa·

ICE REEF

New Guinea: Tribal Areas

Maria-Theresa Reef ○

ABELAM ARAPESH
IATMUL
TANGU
MIMIKA
ASMAT NAMAU
MARIND ANIM ELEMA Goodenough I.
KEREWA
KIWAI
·Aurid
Oenpelli Milingimbi ·Murray
Port
Liverpool R. Bradshaw CAPE YORK PENINSULA

Australia

CHATHAM IS.

2 I

Polynesia

Priests, Poets and Entertainers

Throughout Polynesia much of the creative energy of the people flowed into words that were woven into songs and stories about gods and heroes who had the strengths and weaknesses of men, and into tales of history about noble ancestors who bore the names and attributes of gods. Words were spun by the bards into welcoming orations, love lyrics, laments and eulogies of praise for the great chiefs, warriors and navigators, particularly those who had led the canoe parties to find new lands. Ritual words were guarded by priests, and the master-craftsmen who acted as priests for the canoe-builders, house-builders, fishermen and the makers of images. Prayers summoned gods to the *marae* (temple) and shrines. Invocations, charms and spells used words in formulae so powerful that if any were omitted or misplaced disaster and death followed.

These oral traditions exist wherever the Polynesians settled and on every island the poets, priests and narrators drew from the same deep well of the mythological past which the Polynesians themselves called The Night of Tradition. For when their ancestors moved out from the Polynesian nucleus they carried with them the knowledge of the same great mythological events, the names of their gods and of their many demigods and heroes. As time passed the Polynesian imagination elaborated and adapted old themes to suit fresh settings, and new characters and events were absorbed into the mythological system. But on almost every

island favourite stories have the same central characters: Hina the woman who beat tapa-cloth in the moon; Maui who fished up the islands and snared the sun; Tinirau whose pet whale was murdered by Kae; Tawhaki who visited the sky and Rata whose canoe was built by the little people of the forest.

The action of these stories often took place in Po, the land of darkness or the underworld, and in Hawaiki which, for most of central and eastern Polynesia, was both a land of spirits – sometimes located in the sky – and an ancestral home in the west. In

western Polynesia this place was called Pulotu. In the Hawaiian Islands they spoke of the spirit land of Kahiki (Tahiti) and of The Hidden Land of Kane or the Wandering Isles. Sometimes these could be seen floating offshore or suspended in the sky, but they disappeared if you pointed at them. Sometimes they were situated under the sea. Just as often the action moved between these mythical lands and the familiar setting of the islands themselves.

The pool where Hina met her eel lover was localised on almost every island from Tonga to the Marquesas.

Maui left his footprint on a reef in the Austral Islands and thousands of miles away the people of Manihiki and Rakahanga claim that their tiny atolls were once a single piece of land which broke apart when Maui leapt from it into the heavens. In Hawaii the Wahi Pani or Storied Places are many and well remembered.

The Polynesians lived in a world created by their gods and heroes and felt a close involvement with them. Mythological references like 'as deceitful as Maui' were a part of everyone's conversation. The lullaby for the baby, the story for the curious

Hale-o-Keawe, the temple-mausoleum at Honaunau Bay, Hawaii, is a reconstruction partly based on drawings made by European voyagers. Up to 1818 twenty-two chiefs of the Kona district were buried there and several important images in museum collections come from there. (*See* page 60.) The temple precincts adjoined Pu'uhonua Honaunau, Place of Refuge. Once the 20-acre (8-hectare) enclosure behind the 1,000-foot (304-metre) long massive stone wall was reached, it provided a haven for the defeated in battle and the breakers of *tapu.*

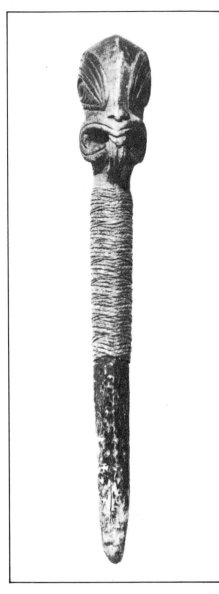

child, the idle tale to pass the time, all drew on the familiar themes. Simple prayers acknowledged the ever-present gods. In Hawaii ordinary men addressed the gods daily, before the meal. The translation is by W. V. Westervelt.

O long god,
O short god,
O god breathing in short sibilant breaths,
O god blowing like the whistling winds!
O god watching, peeping at one!
O god hiding, slipping out of sight
O all ye gods: who travel on the dark night's paths!
Come and eat!

Men also needed more specialised assistance to communicate with their gods. All labour was consecrated. The success of planting, fishing, canoe-making and house-building depended not only on correct technique but also on correct ritual. The master-craftsman of every occupation therefore taught his successor both his technical skills and his collection of spells, invocations, genealogies and legends.

The highest mysteries of traditional lore were the province of the divine chief, the inspirational priest and the ceremonial priest. Every Polynesian chief traced his genealogy back to the gods and was therefore the living link with the mythological past. The inspirational priest was the mouthpiece of the gods, the oracle and diviner, who was consulted before any event of importance. His revelations were probably the source of new myths and the basis for the reinterpretation of the old. The ceremonial priest presided over the public ceremonies associated with the birth, marriage, installation and death of a chief, as well as those which regulated man's association with nature such as the opening of the bird-snaring season of the Maoris, or the turtle-fishing season of the Tuamotuans. Upon him devolved the responsibility of performing the ritual without error. He was also the guardian of the esoteric lore and the teacher of those destined to be chiefs, priests and

bards and he instructed men and women of rank in traditional lore.

Broadly speaking, this was the pattern on most islands, except those of western Polynesia where true ceremonial priests did not exist. There the Talking Chiefs, who were both bards and orators, were the repositories of the traditional lore of the group and simply passed it on from generation to generation.

Elsewhere in Polynesia instruction was formal and took place either in permanent buildings like those of the Whare Wananga or sacred colleges of the Maoris, or in a specially built structure which was later destroyed, like that built by a wealthy Marquesan for the education of his child. Sometimes complete seclusion was demanded during the course of study and strict tapus, including the prohibition of sexual intercourse and restrictions on eating certain foods, were always enforced. The Rarotongans believed that slippery foods like bananas would cause loss of memory while glutinous foods like taro would aid it; the Hawaiians forbade sugar cane because it ruined the voice, and the Marquesan student drank sea foam at his graduation feast to make himself wise.

There were various degrees of learning. In the Society Islands novice priests retired within the sacred enclosures of Houses-in-which-to-absorb-invocations to learn to recite without hesitancy the prayers, chants, invocations and ritual of their profession; and men and women of rank joined a House of Learning to study mythology, genealogy, heraldry, astronomy, navigation and geography, as well as the art of composition. Within the Maori whares eligible young people were instructed in two branches of knowledge, one called Upper Jaw which included everything pertaining to the gods and the origin of things, astronomy, and time-keeping; and the other called Lower Jaw which dealt with the history of migrations, the genealogies and the nature of tapu. The Maoris believed that the god Tane had fetched this knowledge from the highest heavens in three baskets, so the course of study was divided into three parts. It lasted from April to October with daily sessions from sunrise till noon. Tane was also said to have brought with him two stones called Foam-of-the-ocean and White-sea-mist. There were replicas of these in every whare and the students stood on them on graduation day to absorb their mana.

Although this formal education operated as a conservative force in the society, it also provided the framework for consolidating change. It was in the whares of the tribes of the south-east coast of New Zealand that the doctrine of a supreme being, Io, came into being and was nourished. Similarly a famous noble woman, Brave-Hearted, came to Tahiti from the neighbouring island of Ra'iatea, to establish a school, Sacred-cloud-in-the-sky, to spread the doctrine of Oro, god of war, on that island.

The religious festivals and public celebrations which were stage-managed by the hereditary priests and bards also absorbed the energies of the many other people within the group who excelled as musicians, dancers and players. They were required to act as chorus for the sacred ceremonies and they also took part in the lighter entertainments which followed. Naturally these included singing and dancing and dramatic performances, and in the Society Islands and the Hawaiian Islands there were also puppet shows. There were sports events, beauty competitions and riddle contests. The bards, who were in great demand on these occasions, held their own competitions in verse-making. These were serious affairs for a poor performer could even be killed by his fellow bards.

In some archipelagoes the popular entertainers were the young adolescents of the privileged classes, while in the Marquesas the young men who associated together in bands called Ka'ioi were liberally rewarded for their performances at feasts and ceremonies. In times of peace they wandered from village to village as strolling players and minstrels. They rubbed their bodies with perfumed

oils and dyed their skins orange with
tumeric. They adorned themselves
with feather ruffs, anklets and hair
ornaments and wore yellow bark-
cloth garments. Within these informal
groups young men of talent, no
matter how humble their origin,
could achieve social advancement.

In the more class-bound communities of Tahiti and the neighbouring
islands, the loose association of the
ka'ioi was paralleled by the more
formal institution of the Arioi. This
was essentially a cult organisation like
the 'ghost' and 'spirit' societies of
Melanesia which controlled much of
the ceremonial life of that area, but
membership of the Arioi also gave
talented men and women the opportunity to short-circuit the rigid social
divisions for, whatever their social
origin, candidates for the society had
simply to work themselves into a
frenzied state of *nevaneva* and break
into an Arioi performance. Once they
were accepted as novices they were
trained in the art of pantomime and
took part in the comic interludes.
They also performed as a chorus, and

introduced the programme with a
chant praising the attractions of the
district in which they were playing,
its history and its mythological
associations.

There were eight grades of Arioi,
each with its distinctive dress and
tattoo pattern, and members could
advance through successive grades up
to the seventh; but the highest order
of the red tapa girdle (which echoed
the sacred red feather girdle of the
chiefs) could only be inherited. Even
so it could not be assumed automati-
cally; it had to be bestowed by the
high chief himself. Although complete
sexual freedom was permitted and
permanent unions were formed
between members, all grades of the
Arioi, except the highest, had to vow
to destroy all children born to them.
This meant that, in spite of the
personal prestige which they gained
as Arioi, they could never consolidate
their power and thereby threaten the
established hierarchy. Their reward
came after death, when they entered
a special paradise presided over by
the god Roma-Tane.

However, the Arioi were much more than a guild of entertainers, for their artistic skills were dedicated to Oro, whom they called Oro-of-the-laid-down-spear, thus transforming this formidable god of war into a god of peace. Before they set out on a journey they ritually demanded that Oro remain behind at home in the *marae* to safeguard them. One of their number was anointed and garlanded with flowers and this member of the Arioi travelled with them as the incarnation of the god of paradise, Roma-Tane.

The Arioi of the Society Islands were united in what they called The-great-rock-of-the-Arioi. Some idea of the size of the organisation can be gauged from Captain Cook's description of a flotilla of seventy canoes, gay with coloured pennants, spreading bunches of the cock-bird's tail feathers and circular mat sails. On each of these great canoes there was a stage upon which the company acted as they approached the shore. When a party visited another district they were welcomed in the great Arioi houses, some 300 feet (91 metres) long, which had been specially built for them. At night these houses were lit by fires and candlenut tapers which created *rehu arui* (night daylight) and the whole setting was so festive and brimming with happiness that 'even the crickets, it is said, cried with joy on these occasions'.

Very little is known about their performances. The first European witnesses were so shocked by what they regarded as their licentiousness that they recorded no details, and as many of the leading Arioi were amongst the first converts to Christianity, the dissolution of the society was rapid. It is clear however that their pantomimes and acrobatics were not the most important aspect of their performances. That they were fundamentally religious in character was evident to at least one early observer, Consul Moerenhout, who described their performances as 'living pictures' in which they told the story of the creation of all things by the god Tangaroa. This included 'the universe, the gods, the elements,

spirits, plants and other productions of the earth'.

Their purpose was to stimulate fertility in nature, and the burden of such an important function goes a long way towards explaining the tolerance with which the Arioi were received wherever they went. In every district the chiefs and nobility feasted them lavishly and heaped gifts upon them. They remained until the gardens were stripped and the district impoverished. Their privileged position explains how they could, in their entertainments, satirise and ridicule persons of any rank, even priests, without fear. It is said that they acted as instruments of reform.

This role of social commentator was also enjoyed by the Hula troupe of Hawaii who used *ki'i* or marionettes, manipulated by ventriloquists, to tell simple dramatic tales, full of gossip and satirical comment. They were masters of the 'shifty' or double talk. As well as being entertainers they served in a religious capacity at the great public ceremonies like the festival of the first fruits for the god Lono. Laka, the goddess of the wildwood and sister of Lono, was their patroness. Her presence was manifested in a small block of wood which was covered by a piece of yellow tapa and placed on the altar in the special hula house. Garlands of flowers and greenery were brought as offerings. The Hula troupe was neither as

permanent nor as rigid an organisation as the Arioi. Novices and experienced performers came together under a *kumu* who was both leader, teacher and business manager. As his troupers were not food-producers he found a chief to act as patron. Training was strict and surrounded by the usual tapus. Young aspirants were chosen for their beauty, grace, wit and liveliness of imagination. The Rev. Ellis describes the flamboyant appearance of a young Hula trouper: 'His jet-black hair hung in loose and flowing ringlets – his necklace was made of a vast number of strings of nicely braided human hair – an ornament made from a whale's tooth hung pendant from it on his breast; his wrists were ornamented with bracelets formed of the polished tusks of the hog, and his ankles with loose buskins set with dog's teeth, the rattle of which, during the dance, kept time with the music of the calabash drum. A beautiful yellow tapa was tastefully fastened round his loins, reaching to his knees.'

The contrast between these vivacious entertainers and the solemn and dignified priests and bards was tremendous, but together they were guardians of the traditional lore and through them the Polynesians consciously preserved and transmitted the esoteric truths enshrined in their mythology.

A Maori priest invokes a god represented by a carved godstock. As he chanted he tugged the string to attract the god's attention. (*See* page 24.) Engraving from *New Zealand and its Inhabitants* by Richard Taylor.

Creation of the Cosmos

Amongst the Polynesians genesis was conceived of as either a process of growth or evolution from an intangible to a tangible state, or as the work of a pre-existent, omniscient creator who brought matter into existence, gave form to the formless and set all in an established order. The primordial state in which the creator dwelt or from which all things emerged was described as a Void, Nothingness, Chaos, Immensity, Space, Night or Darkness, and in an attempt to free the concept even more it was qualified as limitless, without light, without form or without motion. The Void was divided into the First Void, the Second Void, the Far-Extending Void, the Vast, and the Unpossessed. The aeons of Darkness or *Po* were Extreme, Black, Gloomy and Never-ending.

The belief in a pre-existent creator, called Tangaloa, who lived alone in the Illimitable Void and made all things, was found in the western Polynesian islands of the Samoan, Tongan and Tuvaluan groups and on Niue, Uvea and Rotuma. Tangaloa, some said, brooded over a vast expanse of waters while his messenger, the bird Tuli, flew over the never-ending oceans searching for somewhere to rest. At last Tangaloa cast down a rock which became the island of Manu'a, the main island of the Samoan group. Next he made the other islands of the group, then Tonga and Fiji. Tuli complained of the lack of shade in those islands and Tangaloa gave him a vine to plant called the Peopling Vine, from which man was made.

An evolutionary type of creation story was more characteristic of central and eastern Polynesia. Very often it was expressed in genealogical terms beginning with the union of the passive element of *Po*, darkness, and the active element of *Ao*, light. Sometimes the successive stages of creation were expressed almost entirely in abstract terms, as in the Maori creation chant collected by the Rev. R. Taylor, which begins:

From the conception the increase,
From the increase the swelling,
From the swelling the thought,
From the thought the remembrance,
From the remembrance the
consciousness, the desire.

Such a hypnotic flow of words suggests that the chant had a ritual purpose.

Other creation myths of the evolutionary type were completely personalised. The two elements became an earth mother and a sky father, who were the progenitors of the gods, the elements, the lands and all living things. In myths of this type the first-born sons of the primal pair played an active part in creation: separating their parents, raising the sky and creating lands, plants and man. The names and the attributes of the greatest of these, the gods Tane, Tangaroa, Tu and Rongo were known throughout almost all of Polynesia except the west, where Tangaroa or Tangaloa alone was known, not as one of the pantheon of great gods, but as sole creator.

A personalised account of creation

Above Tahitian godhouse (fare atua) or 'ark' in the shape of a pig, in which sacred objects – small images, ceremonial regalia or feathers – could be stored on the marae or transported. This one is about three feet (a metre) in length. Museum of Mankind, London.

Left Image of the god, A'a, from Rurutu in the Austral Islands. The figure has a cavity in its back which once held a number of smaller images, now lost. Museum of Mankind, London.

Left The separation of the primal pair. Papa, Earth Mother, and Rangi, Sky Father, are depicted on a barge board or *maihi* of the Maori meeting house, Te Mana o Turanganui-o-Kiwa at Whakato near Manutuke, east coast, North Island, New Zealand.

was given to Sir George Grey by the chief of the Arawa tribe of New Zealand. It begins with the statement: 'Men had but one pair of primitive ancestors; they sprang from the vast heaven that exists above us, and from the earth which lies beneath us.' They were called Rangi and Papa and '. . . they still both clave together'. Because of this '. . . there was darkness from the first division of time unto the tenth, to the hundredth, to the thousandth, that is for a vast space of time'. These divisions of time were considered as beings and were each termed a Po. Within the warm embrace of Papa and Rangi lay the beings they had already created, including the gods Tane, Tangaroa, Tu, Rongo, Haumia and Tawhiri. The offspring of Rangi and Papa became restless within their cramped quarters and debated whether they should kill their parents or rend them apart.

Tu-of-the-angry-face cried, 'Let us slay them.' But Tane, father of the forests and creatures of the forest, argued, 'It is better to rend them apart, and let heaven stand far above us, and the earth lie under our feet.' All the brothers agreed with him except Tawhiri, father of storms and winds, who grieved at the thought of separating his parents. The argument raged in the darkness until at last they determined to act and each son in

his turn tried to separate the parents. Rongo, father of cultivated foods, tried first; then Tangaroa, father of fishes and reptiles, followed by Haumia, father of uncultivated plants and then Tu. All failed. Finally Tane tried but his arms were too short, so placing his head against his mother, the earth, and raising his feet against his father, the sky, he strained and struggled to separate them. He took no heed of their wailing protests as he gradually pressed down the earth and thrust up the sky.

Tawhiri bitterly resented his brothers' treatment of their parents and rising, clung to the vast heaven and plotted revenge. First he sent his offspring, the four great winds, to the east, the west, the south and the north. Next he sent forth '. . . fierce squalls, whirlwinds, dense clouds, massy clouds, dark clouds, gloomy thick clouds, fiery clouds which precede the hurricanes; in fact all sorts of storm clouds'. He snapped the great trees of the forests of Tane and lashed the seas of Tangaroa whose progeny panicked and separated. 'The fish fled in confusion to the sea, the reptiles sought safety in the forests and scrubs.' Tangaroa was enraged at some of his children deserting him and sheltering in the forests of Tane. These two brothers have quarrelled ever since. Hence Tane supplies the offspring of his

Opposite A puppet from Hawaii, made of light wood covered with black tapa cloth. Its arms are moveable and six teeth serve as fingers, its upper teeth are human and the lower are palatine teeth of a fish. Museum of Mankind, London.

31

Above A carved wooden figure, possibly of the god Rongo, from Mangareva. It is one of seven images known to have survived a mass destruction of carvings which took place on April 16, 1835, at the instigation of the missionaries. Metropolitan Museum of Art, New York.

Right In Hawaii these grotesque wooden images scowled down on the proceedings within the *heiau* or sacred precincts. This one was removed from the *haeiau* of Kawailae dedicated to Ku, at Kailau, Hawaii. Museum of Mankind, London.

brother Tu with canoes, with spears, and with fish-hooks made from his trees and nets woven from his fibrous plants, that they may destroy the offspring of Tangaroa, whilst Tangaroa, in return, swallows up the offspring of Tane. 'He overwhelms canoes, trees, lands and houses and ever wastes away, with his lapping waves, the shores that confine him.'

The brothers Rongo and Haumia hid themselves in Mother Earth to escape Tawhiri's wrath. The latter turned his anger against Tu who not only withstood his passionate assaults but defeated him. Then Tu in his turn sought to take revenge on his brothers for deserting him in battle. He fashioned snares to trap the birds of Tane's forests and made nets from flax plants to enmesh the children of Tangaroa. He pulled up by the hair (leaves) the children of Haumia and Rongo and left them to dry in the sun. He consumed all his brothers' progeny as food. Tu bore the likeness of man and assumed many names: Tu-the-lover-of-war, Tu-the-man-consumer and Tu-of-the-narrow-face. Tu learnt many incantations to control his brothers; incantations for food and possessions, for favourable winds and weather and also '. . . for Mother Earth that she might produce all things abundantly'.

During the time of Tawhiri's wrath much of the dry land was submerged by '. . .Terrible rain. Long-continued rain, Fierce-hailstorms; and their progeny, Mist, Heavy-dew and Light-dew'. Afterwards clear light increased upon the earth and all the beings who had been hidden between Papa and Rangi multiplied. Ever since then Papa and Rangi have dwelt apart, but her loving sighs still rise up to him as mist and his tears fall as dew drops.

The flood motif which occurs in this myth is sometimes touched on in the creation stories of other islands. There is a hint of it in those that describe a primal expanse of waters and also in the Kumulipo creation chant of Hawaii where it is implied that the primary state of chaos is the result of the wreck and ruin of an earlier world. There is also a Samoan story about a primeval octopus whose

children are Fire and Water. Their offspring fight a great battle and everything is overwhelmed by a 'boundless sea', and the god Tangaloa has the task of re-creating the world.

The Maori view of creation in which all nature was seen as a great kinship tracing its origins back to a single pair, the Sky Father and the Earth Mother, was a conception which they brought with them when they came from central Polynesia about A.D. 1000. Furthermore this belief in a primal pair, as well as the metaphysical idea of an original Void or Darkness, seems to be part of the stock of ideas which the ancestors of the Polynesians brought with them from the west, from Southeast Asia and which they carried with them as they dispersed into marginal Polynesia. The resultant shift in names and attributes, and the elaboration of themes which occurred throughout the area, cannot obscure this underlying unity of ideas. The Sky Father, known as Rangi to the Maoris, was called Atea Rangi by the Tuamotuans, and Atea, which means 'great expanse of sky' or light, was the name most commonly given him elsewhere in eastern Polynesia. The male force was also known as Te Tumu, the source or cause. Papa, which means earth foundation, was the most usual name for the Earth Mother but sometimes, especially on coral atolls like those of the Tuamotuan chain, the female element was known as Fakahotu or Hakahotu, names which suggest coral growth.

Although the Mangaian islanders of the Cook group believed that Vatea (Atea) and Papa were the progenitors of gods and men, they did not know Vatea as the Sky Father but as one of the six children which Vari-ma-te-takere, the Beginning-and-the-bottom, plucked from her side. He was formed half-fish, half-man. The Mangaians believed that the universe was contained within a vast coconut shell, called Avaiki (Hawaiki), and at the very bottom dwelt Vari, a self-existent being. Vari also means mud, and in the sense of an original chaos of mud from which life grew this Mangaian belief rather resembles that

of the original state of chaos postulated in the myths of other islands. Below Vari, and contained within the tapered point of the stem of the coconut, was the threadlike Root-of-all-existence, Take, and the whole universe was said to be constantly sustained from that point. Above Vari were the various strata allocated to gods and men.

This idea of an initial kernel of life being enclosed within a spherical primal form is found elsewhere in Polynesia; sometimes it is represented as an egg, sometimes as a shell. Early European recorders of Tuamotuan and Mangaian creation myths illustrated them in diagrams which showed the various planes of earth and a series of skies contained within the sphere. But perhaps these charts give too concrete a form to an idea which the Polynesians themselves meant only as a metaphor, for in a myth from the Society Islands it was explained that as Ta'aroa (Tangaroa), the creator, has a shell '. . . so everything has a shell. The sky is a shell that is endless space . . . man's shell is woman . . . woman's shell is woman. . . . One cannot enumerate the shells of all the things that this world produces'.

In this particular myth, which was related by Teuira Henry in *Ancient Tahiti*, Ta'aroa was acclaimed as the originator of all things, and embellishments of the plot apparently serve to justify his promotion to this position.

In the beginning, it was said that Ta'aroa developed himself in solitude; he was his own parent and he dwelt quite alone in his shell which had the name Rumia – Upset. 'The shell was like an egg revolving in endless space, with no sky, no land, no sea, no moon, no sun, no stars.' At last Ta'aroa gave his shell a flip and slipped out, but all was silent and dark and he was alone. He retreated to a new shell and spent many aeons in contemplation. At last he took the new shell to be a foundation and the old to be the dome of a sky. He identified himself with Te Tumu, the Source, and began the task of creation. Within the darkness he

33

Hawaiian feather image of the type sometimes referred to as Kukailimoku, Ku snatcher of lands, a god of war. The feathers have been twined into a netted support over a basketwork frame. Museum of Mankind, London.

The reply was: 'A clod of earth. A huge jellyfish. A shapeless nothing.'

It was Ta'aroa who summoned the artisans with their baskets of adzes to fashion him into 'a good-looking boy'. Again it was Ta'aroa who exalted Tane and gave him the tenth or highest heaven as his dwelling place. Tane retained the leading part however in raising the skies and this version of the myth provides one of the most colourful elaborations of this theme.

Although Rua, the Abyss, managed to conjure to death the great spotted octopus that held heaven and earth together the beast did not release its hold, and life continued within the confined darkness. The demi-gods were born. Rû-who-explored-the-earth and Hina-who-stepped-into-the-moon and the eight-headed Maui were amongst their number. First Rû tried to raise Atea, the sky. He lifted him as high as the broad leaves of the arrowroot plant and then to the top of a tall coral tree, but the strain was so great that he became humpbacked and ruptured himself so badly that his intestines floated away and settled as clouds above the island of Borabora. At length Maui took up the task and set wedges in the gaps between heaven and earth and fixed props to support the great weight of the sky. Then he flew to the highest heaven to seek the help of Tane.

That god took his basket of flashing shell adzes and his pet white swallow, and descended to earth. He used great logs as props and levers and began to bore into Atea with his shells. Atea cried out in pain but Tane went on digging and boring until at last Atea was freed and light came into the world. There was a rolling and tumbling as the gods fell over themselves with joy at their release. The arms of the octopus became detached and fell away to become the island of Tabua'i, in the Austral group.

The coming of light revealed much that was ugly; the crooked, the blind and those suffering from elephantiasis. Gradually the heavens became clear and Tane decorated them with the stars and set the sun and the moon

called the gods into being. He shook his feathers (red and yellow feathers were supposed to clothe the gods in the beginning) and as they fell they made '. . . trees, plantain clusters and verdure upon the land'. All this was done in a confined world because the sky was still held down upon the earth by the great arms of the Octopus, Tumu-ra'i-feuna, Foundation-of-earthly-heaven.

Ta'aroa's supremacy over other gods, particularly Tane, was stressed. At Tane's birth it was asked: 'Did you notice whom he resembles?'

in their courses. Everything was given its appointed place. The turtle and the seal, with the whale, the shark and other great fish were to swim in the sea; the turtle was to lay its eggs in the sand and the salmon was to leap in the rivers and the sea in its season. No detail was neglected. Even the god Tohu, of the Chasms-of-the-deep, was appointed '. . . to paint in perfect, gorgeous colours the fishes and shells of the deep'.

Even in a world made by Ta'aroa, Tane's role as life-creator could not be dismissed but it was qualified, for the chant concluded: 'This then was Tane; he was a very great god. Ta'aroa made him great, and all his greatness emanated from Ta'aroa.'

Apparently this elevation of Ta'aroa reflected the victory of his worshippers over the worshippers of other gods. It is difficult to say when in historical time this might have taken place but it must have been a late development because the belief in Ta'aroa's supremacy had not spread much beyond the Society Islands and some of the Tuamotus by the time of the first European contacts, and even there it existed side by side with other variants. Such a movement must certainly have been stimulated, if not actually started, by a chief called Tu who became Pomare I shortly after Captain Cook visited the Society Islands, for Pomare traced his descent from Ta'aroa and he probably used his political victories to establish his family deity as a national god.

Cook Island traditions provide the corollary to this story for they tell of the arrival of Tahitian refugees who were worshippers of Tane. Before leaving Tahiti the priest placed a piece of finely plaited sennit, symbol of Tane-the-artisan, in a coconut shell container and set it adrift on the ocean. He followed later in a canoe, searching for it. At length it was recovered in the lagoon of Mangaia. When the stopper was withdrawn the god chirped and so was named Tane-the-chirper. The Mangaians already worshipped Tane-the-artisan, and made beautiful basaltic adzes lashed to the haft with fine sennit braiding, to represent him. They were not

One of several rare free-standing Maori images. Human hair was attached to the figure's scalp. Glasgow Art Gallery and Museum.

35

impressed by Tane-the-chirper. The affronted priest carried his god off to the island of Aitutaki.

The Mangaians who, tradition suggests, came from Rarotonga, had recast their myths in several ways. They acknowledged Tangaroa as the first-born son of Atea and Papa but as they traced their descent from Rongo, the second son, they gave him precedence over Tangaroa. They explained that this had come about because Papa, who favoured Rongo, had cunningly suggested that all the foods which were red in colour and therefore sacred should belong to Tangaroa; all the rest should go to Rongo. This meant that Rongo got the greater part and became rich and Tangaroa was forced to leave Mangaia and go in search of other lands. The Mangaians also took their Rarotongan ancestor, the great chief Tangiia, and deified him. Projecting him back in time, they set him in their pantheon of gods as brother of Rongo and Tangaroa.

It has been suggested that a similar process of deification of a great ancestral chief, priest or navigator was the way in which the Polynesians made their gods. It could certainly apply to the apotheosis of local gods in competition with the older ones, but it does not seem a satisfactory explanation of the origin of the classic gods of the Polynesian pantheon, for these were so widely known that they must have acquired their names and attributes somewhere in the Polynesian heartland before dispersal. In the creation stories each god presided over his own department of nature and it was through an appeal to each of them in these special roles that man controlled the forces of nature. In this function lies the clue to their origin.

Gods Work for Man

Tu

Tu's name means 'to stand' and 'to strike' and he was a god of war to whom human sacrifices were made. The idea of stability which his name also implied was reflected in his role as assistant to Ta'aroa, the creator, in the myths of the Society Islands, and in those islands his warlike aspect was adopted by Oro, a son of Ta'aroa. In New Zealand there was a multitude of local war gods. In Hawaii, where he was known as Ku-of-the-deep-forest, Ku-of-the-undergrowth, Ku-adzing-out-the-canoe, he was also the patron of wood-workers; but he was also known as Ku-the-snatcher-of-lands and Ku-with-the-maggot-dropping-mouth, who received human sacrifices. The family of gods classed as Ku were formidable gods of war in Hawaii.

Rongo

Rongo was known as Ono in the Marquesas and Lono in Hawaii. His name means 'sound' and the Mangaians represented him by a great triton shell called The Resounder. In the Marquesas he was patron of singing but his principle association was with cultivated foods. As Lono in the Hawaiian Islands he was god of agriculture and was said to have introduced the Makahiki rite, a harvest festival that was a time of singing and celebration. The high priest was blindfolded for five days of merrymaking and the people indulged in wrestling matches and other sports. The Long God, an upright pole with a cross piece from which hung feather wreaths and long streamers of tapa, was carried in a circuit of the island. Wherever it rested tribute was exacted, and when it returned to the ruling chief's district he sailed out to meet it. When he landed a spear was thrown at him which was parried by a special attendant. A mock battle followed. The following day there was feasting and the Net of Maoleha, a large meshed net full of food, was shaken out. If no food clung to the net, this meant that a season of plenty was certain.

Lono was invoked by a prayer, which is given here in David Malo's version:

Oh Lono shake out a net-full of food,
A net-full of rain.
Gather them together for us.
Accumulate food, Oh Lono!
Collect fish, Oh Lono!
Wauke shoots and colouring matter
* for tapa.*

Wauke shoots are those of the paper mulberry, from which tapa cloth is made. The mythological explanation of the Makahiki was that Lono descended on a rainbow to find a mortal wife. At first they were very happy together but one day he was led to believe that she had been unfaithful so he beat her to death. Then in his grief and anguish he instituted games in her honour and travelled about the island issuing challenges to wrestle. Afterwards he sailed away on a special canoe laden with provisions, promising to return on a floating island, abundant with food. When Captain Cook arrived the islanders identified him with the returning Lono.

Tane

Tane, known as Kane in Hawaii, signifies 'man'. He fulfilled many great tasks: separating earth and sky, beautifying the heavens and creating woman. Tane's life-giving qualities were symbolised in myth and prayer as The-water-of-life-of-Tane. He was lord of the forest and all the creatures who lived in it. All who used wood, particularly the canoe-builders, invoked him. In the Society Islands they prayed to him before they 'put their axes to sleep' in a niche in the temple on the night before they used them, and again in the morning when they 'woke' their axes in the sea. T. Henry has recorded the song they chanted when they lashed the planking of the canoe together. They sang

What have I, O Tane,
Tane, God of beauty!
'Tis sennit.
'Tis sennit, of the host of heaven,
'Tis sennit for thee, O Tane!
Thread it from the inside, it comes
* outside,*
Thread it from the outside, it goes
* inside.*
Tie it firmly, bind it fast.

Tangaroa

In the outer regions of Polynesia Tangaroa was the god of the ocean and of fishermen. In central Polynesia he was sometimes promoted to the position of creator. In western Polynesia he was the pre-existent creator whose sole domain was the high heavens. There he was also patron of house-builders and carpenters, for the first house was built in heaven. Hawaiian tradition stated specifically that Kane and Kanaloa, as they were known there, came from Kahiki (Tahiti) and as old gods were not considered very important. Hawaii, almost more than anywhere else in Polynesia, possessed a proliferation of gods.

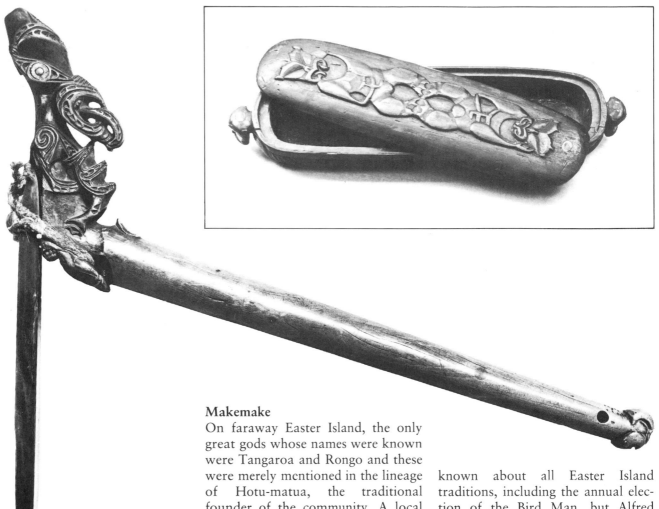

Above A Maori chief's ceremonial adze with greenstone blade. University Museum, Philadelphia, Pennsylvania.

Above right A Maori box from Urewera district, North Island, for storing feathers and other small precious objects. National Museum of New Zealand, Wellington, ex Buller Collection.

Opposite The upper portion of a Rarotongan staff god of which the flattened head surmounts a series of figures, alternatively profile and full-face. Usually only this carved section survived (*see* page 17), but below it the middle section would have been wrapped round with tapa cloth with the end terminating in a phallus. According to the missionary, John Williams, pieces of polished pearl shell and red feathers were placed within the tapa roll to represent the soul of the god. Museum of Mankind, London.

Makemake

On faraway Easter Island, the only great gods whose names were known were Tangaroa and Rongo and these were merely mentioned in the lineage of Hotu-matua, the traditional founder of the community. A local god, Makemake, usurped the function of Tane as creator of mankind and was also patron of the Bird Cult, the principle festival of the island. He first manifested himself in the form of a skull and the large-eyed rock-carvings or petroglyphs at the sacred village of Orongo are said to represent him. This village was built on the cliffs overlooking three small islets and it was to one of these, Motu-nui, that Makemake was said to have driven the birds to protect them from the egg gatherers.

Each year in the nesting season, servants were sent to the island to await the appearance of the first egg, while their masters waited at Orongo. The man whose servant found the first egg became Bird Man, for one year. His hair and eyebrows were shaved and his eyelashes cut off and he carried the egg on the palm of his hand down the mountain to a place where he lived in seclusion for the rest of the year. Tantalisingly little is known about all Easter Island traditions, including the annual election of the Bird Man, but Alfred Métraux, scholar of Easter Island culture, suggests that the Bird Man was the chosen representative of Makemake and that the contest for fetching the first egg determined his selection.

Io-the-hidden-face: Io-the-originator-of-all-things

About the middle of last century certain Maori priests of some of the east coast tribes were consecrating classes in their schools of sacred learning with prayers to Io-the-self-created, a god unknown elsewhere in Polynesia. His presence at the head of the hierarchy of Maori gods was unknown until the 1870s when the first European reference to him was published. Most of our knowledge about him comes from *The Lore of the Whare Wananga*. Although this was not translated and published until this century it was formulated during the 1860s from the teachings of two Maori priests, Te Matoro-

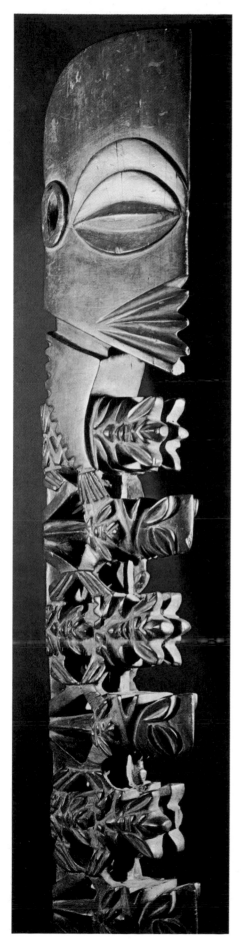

hanga and Nepia Pohuhu. Not only was it written down by Maori 'scribes', but the finer doctrinal points were also thrashed out by a committee of Maori priests and elders. *The Lore* explicitly stated that '... the priests alone had complete knowledge of Io and that ordinary people knew nothing'.

This could be interpreted as meaning either that the inner knowledge had been deliberately withheld, or that the cult of Io represented a reorganisation of Maori sacred lore. Some of Io's names certainly seem to be derived from Christianity, for as well as being Io-of-the-hidden-face, that is, not manifested in material form, he was also called Io-eternal and Io-god-of-love. He was said to have created all things by 'The Word'. But although the priests had revised the esoteric lore to establish Io in a position of supremacy he was not made a solitary deity. The pantheon remained. Two more heavens were added to the ten of earlier creation stories, and Io was accommodated in the highest. Tane was assigned a new task; after separating Rangi and Papa he ascended to Io and asked him for the three baskets which contained all knowledge, especially that 'pertaining to the Sky Father and the Earth Mother'.

The doctrine of Io was much more than an attempt to amalgamate Christian and Maori beliefs. Io manifested himself at a time of Maori resurgence and the tale of this Io-of-all-knowledge was to re-enforce the validity of the old beliefs with the sanction of a supreme deity who would match the Christian god.

The Origin of Mankind

Tuli, the bird messenger of Tangaloa, flew down to earth with a creeping vine to clothe the bare land and provide shade. At first the vine spread; then it withered and decomposed and swarmed with a shapeless moving mass of maggots. Tangaloa took these and fashioned them into human shape. He straightened them out and moulded hands, legs and

features. He gave each a heart and a soul and they came alive. This type of myth in which man appeared by a kind of primitive evolution, sometimes aided by a deity, was confined to the western Polynesians.

In the other islands to the east it was believed that man came into being by a continuation of the process of creation, or rather procreation, which had begun with Atea and Papa. The god Tane was most often considered to be the actual generative agent who impregnated a woman he formed from earth. In Maori lore Tane's procreative power and organ was called Tiki. In other places, including the Marquesas, Tiki or Ti'i (Ki'i in Hawaii) was a separate character who replaced Tane as creator of the first woman.

Tane, the Earth-formed-Maiden and the Dawn-Maiden

The Maori story of Tane's search for a wife as told to John White, is that first he turned to his mother, Papa, who rejected him. Then he united with several different beings, but each time their offspring were things like mountain streams, reptiles, rush-like grass and stones. This did not satisfy Tane, who bore the likeness of a man. He longed to have a partner to match himself. At last he took his mother's advice and formed the shape of a woman out of the soft red sand of the seashore of Hawaiki. He breathed life into her nostrils, ears, mouth and eyes. Hot breath burst from her mouth and she sneezed. She opened her eyes and she saw Tane. Her name was Hine-hau-one, the Earth-formed-maiden. Their first child was called Hine-titama, the Dawn-maiden. After a while Tane took the Dawn-maiden as his wife. The girl did not know that Tane was her father as well as her husband. When she asked who her father was she was told to '... ask that question of the pillars of the house'. Hine did so but the house-posts did not answer nor did the side panels. Then the Dawn-maiden realised the truth. She fled in shame from Hawaiki to the darkness of Po, the underworld. When Tane tried to follow her she cried out to him that she had ' . . . cut the cord of this world' and that he must return to look after their children in the world of light while she remained in the world of darkness to drag their children down. This was the origin of death. Hine-titama, Dawn-maiden, became Hine-nui-te-Po, Great-goddess-of-darkness.

In this story Hine, or Hina as she is called in other places, has a dual nature. She is presented as both the first woman and as a goddess who is guardian of the land of the dead. She is both a life-giver and life-destroyer.

Sometimes the name Ti'i was given, not to the creator, but to the first man. The Tahitians believed that Ta'aroa made Ti'i, 'the very first man in the world' as a husband for 'Hina the goddess, who was the first woman in the world'. She was also called Hina-the-mitigator-of-many-things and Hina-who-ate-from-before-and-behind (because she had two faces). They had many children, some of whom were called Hina also, who intermarried with the gods. The rigid class divisions of Tahitian society were also explained in the same myth. Great chiefs or 'royalty' (a European term adopted in the 19th century) were the direct descendants of Ti'i and Hina, while the common people were simply 'conjured' into being by them. 'When the royal family espoused the common people they begat the gentry of the world. When the royal family espoused the gentry they begat the nobility of the world.' The royal family's status was marked by the 'ura girdle'. This girdle, which was the symbolic umbilical cord binding gods and men, was made of sacred red feathers that were lock-stitched into holes made in a fine tapa backing. The sacred needle of human bone was never taken out of the work because it was meant to continue for ever, a new section being added for each successive reign. A human sacrifice was demanded for the first putting in of the needle and two more were required in the course of the work. One such girdle belonging to a chiefly family of Ra'iatea was 21 feet (6.4 metres) long and six inches (15 centimetres) wide.

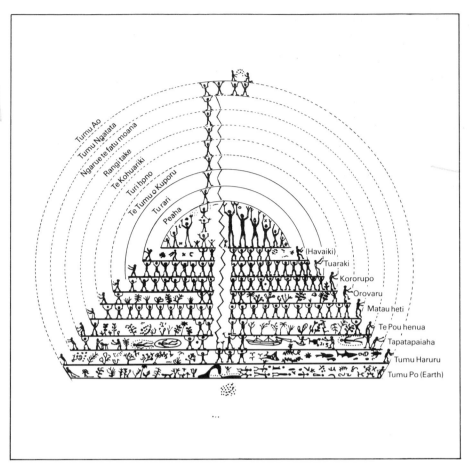

The unions between the gods and human beings which took place long ago in the mythological past tended to blur the line between divine and human ancestors in the genealogies of men. Many men also counted amongst their ancestors the children of such unions, the demi-gods and heroes whose adventures were performed when the world was young and the journey could still be made between the world of the living and the spirit lands, aided by the power of their divine relatives. Their deeds were eulogised in narrative, drama, poetry and song and the names of some were known almost more widely than those of the gods. The most famous and well-loved was certainly Maui-of-a-thousand-tricks who helped the gods to complete the work of putting the world in order and brought many benefits to mankind. Another was Tinirau whose character displayed both a charming and a sinister aspect; he was also associated with faithful sea creatures. There was also the noble Tawhaki who faced many supernatural perils

to rescue his dishonoured father; and his grandson, the honest and impulsive Rata, who in spite of his brash behaviour, was helped by the gods in building his canoe.

The need of every man of status for a famous ancestor resulted in the absorption of these characters into the genealogies of the ruling Polynesian families, and when more than one of them appeared in the same genealogy, brought them also into relationship with each other. Sometimes however, relationships between heroes were established in another way. A characteristic of Polynesian oral literature is the tendency for additional incidents and stories to become attached to a basic core or plot centred on one character. In this way, in eastern Polynesia, the incident of Hina and her eel lover was often included in the cycle of stories about Maui's adventures, with all the change in emphasis and characterisation that such a shift demands. The stories of Tawhaki and Rata were almost always associated in a great cycle of tales involving successive

A Tuamotuan cosmology, expressed diagrammatically, has at the base-centre the hook symbol of Te Tumu, the Source, and the flat black symbolising Te Papa, the Stratum Rock. Above them are the ten layers of creation; each horizontal layer of earth has its accompanying arc of sky. The inner plane of earth being Fakahotu with Atea, Sky, arched above. (Neither are named on the diagram.) In the tenth sky Tangaroa-i-te-Po is being restrained from setting fire to the skies. After K. P. Emory's interpretation of the Paiore-Caillet chart in the Bernice P. Bishop Museum, Honolulu. (*See* p. 33.)

generations in which the same motifs shifted from one character to another in the different versions in a bewildering fashion. Each story or cycle of stories had its supporting cast and in many of them, with the frequency of a refrain, there appeared a character called Hina, who was sometimes a woman and sometimes a goddess.

Hina – The Universal Woman

The different facets of Hina's personality were most often revealed by her composite names. She was most closely associated with the moon, and although she rarely received the worship accorded male gods, Hina-of-the-moon was invoked in the fertility ceremonies of the firewalkers of Ra'iatea as Hina-of-the-scented herbs; a name which probably derived from the garlands and wreaths of sweet-smelling green and yellow ti leaves she and her companion, the Great-woman-who-set-fire-to-the-sky, were said to have worn. Her companion resembles Pele, the Hawaiian goddess of volcanic fires, in that both were said to

command the lightning. As such she seems to be another aspect of Hina herself, for the Hawaiians say that Pele's human incarnation was Hina-ai-malama or Hina-who-eats-the-moon.

There are many explanations of how Hina came to be in the moon. The Tahitians told of Hina-the-canoe-pilot who sailed with her brother Rû in *The Hull* on a great voyage of discovery. Then one evening when the moon was full she sailed off on her own to visit it. She liked it so much she set her canoe adrift and stayed there. She became Hina-the-watchwoman, guardian of travellers. When the moon is bright she can be seen making bark cloth or tapa from the numerous branches of the banyan tree the shape of which can be seen in the shadows on the moon. For this reason she was also known as Hina-the-tapa-beater, and as such was patroness of womanly crafts, particularly the making of tapa. On one occasion she broke off a branch of the tree with such force that it fell through space and landed near the sacred temple of Opoa, Ra'iatea, where it took root and became the first banyan tree in the world.

Others say Hina stepped into the moon because of an argument with Tangaroa. Apparently she beat her tapa cloth with such vigour that Tangaroa, who was suffering the effects of too much kava drinking, found the noise unbearable and sent messengers asking her to stop. She refused. He asked her again, and again, and each time she refused. Furious, Tangaroa ordered the messenger to go back and hit her on the head with her own mallet. The blow was so violent that her spirit left her body and ascended to the moon. She went on working there. Her role as tapa-beater may have more sombre connotations. The Mangaians forbade the beating of tapa during a period of mourning because they believed that a spirit of the underworld who had taught woman tapa-beating would be offended. The stroke of her tapa-beater represented the stroke of death. It seems probable

therefore that Hina-the-tapa-beater represented yet another side of Great-Hina-of-the-darkness who brought death to mankind.

Hina's place for beating cloth was localised on many islands. On Ra'iatea, not far inland, there was a long stone which was said to represent the trunk of the breadfruit tree she used for making the finest white cloth. The Hawaiians believed that a certain long black rock, visible above the surf-line, at a spot on the island of Maui, was where she worked. Stories from that district described her both as the mother of Maui and the ancestress of Kaha'i (Tawhaki) and Laka (Rata), who returned to the moon after a difference with her husband. Another Hawaiian view occurred in the Kumulipo chant where she was described as a mysterious undersea woman. The version is by David Kalakaua.

Hina-who-worked-in-the-moon
  floated as a Bailer
Was taken into the canoe, hence
  called Hina-the-Bailer,
Carried to the shore and put by the
  fire,
Coral insects were born, the eel was
  born,
The sea-urchin was born, the sea-egg
  was born,
The black stone was born, the
  volcanic stone was born,
Hence she was called Hina-from-
  whose-womb-came-various-
  forms.

The Hawaiians attributed these procreative powers of Hina to yet another person called Haumea, mother of Pele. Sometimes they identified Haumea with the first woman who they called not Hina but La'ila'i. Or again Haumea was incarnated in human form as Papa, the wife of Wakea (Atea), but in Hawaii, Papa and Wakea were not the primal pair, they were the first ancestors of the island chiefs. Hina-the-Bailer was Wakea's second wife, after Haumea. This tangle of relationships strengthens the impression that all these various female characters really represent aspects of one being who

acted as both a creative and destructive force.

This dual nature of woman as set out in *The Lore of the Whare Wananga*, was that 'each thing has its female through which it conceives' but 'it is the mana of the female organ' which destroys.

This referred to the belief that 'femaleness' could pollute man's relationship with the sacred; conversely contact with things sacred could endanger woman. This did not necessarily mean a woman lacked freedom or status, but it did mean that her activities were restricted. She was segregated during menstruation and childbirth. In some places she could not eat with the men – whose food was prepared with different utensils and cooked in different ovens. A Marquesan woman could not even set foot in a canoe for fear of contaminating it. Anything tainted by contact with her could easily cause illness or death or be used in sorcery. The resulting aborted or miscarried embryos then became the demons of this world.

Haumea, the Creator

The Hawaiians regarded Haumea as the patroness of childbirth because she was said to have introduced natural childbirth. Before her women were cut open to deliver a child. As a reward she was granted the name 'tree of changing leaves' or 'tree of Never-ending-vegetable-food-supply'. In some versions it was from this tree that Makalei came – the stick which had the power to attract fish. The Hawaiians used a charred oiled bstick for just such a purpose.

Haumea used the stick of Makalei to transform herself from an old woman to a budding girl. The Kumu-lipo chant explains the reasons for these transformations.

Many bodies had this woman Haumea,
Great Haumea was wonderful,
Wonderful was Haumea in the way she lived;
She lived with her grandchildren,
She slept with her children . . .

until she was found out and then:

Haumea was recognised as withered up,
She was old, she was not desired . . .
She stamped on the ground, left Nu'umea
The earth shook, the woman ceased living with many husbands. . .

Nu'umea was one of the several heavens.

Haumea possessed powerful magic. She was said to have saved her husband Wakea from being sacrificed by passing through the trunk of a breadfruit tree with him and escaping. As they fled the fragments torn from her skirt changed into morning glory flowers.

But Haumea the great producer sometimes used her powers destructively. Some say she withdrew the wild plants of the forest which people relied on when cultivated foods were

scarce. A trickster, Kaulu, whose name means 'growth in plants' (particularly the breadfruit), broke her power by stealing cultivated plants from the gods and killed her by tossing her in the net of Maoleha. This was the net of divination in which food was tossed each year at the Makahiki ceremony.

Haumea's control over uncultivated foods indicates her relationship to Haumia, the father of uncultivated foods in the Maori stories.

Pele, the Destroyer

Pele, the Hawaiian goddess of volcanic fires, symbolised woman at her most destructive. Like many other beings of Polynesian myth she was a great voyager. She was said to have come from Kahiki (Tahiti). Some say she was driven out by her elder sister whose husband she stole, or that she

Above Numerous carvings of the bird-man, some showing him with egg in hand, were made on the cliff top at Orongo on Easter Island. Each year the first egg was kept by the birdman. After three days the shell was emptied and filled with tapa. It had the power to increase the food supply.

Opposite Rarotongan ironwood image, collected by the London Missionary Society and labelled 'Te Rongo and his three sons'. There seems some doubt about this, as Te Rongo is not known to have had three sons, although nearby Mangaian Islanders say that Rongo had three sons who were ancestors of the Ngariki tribe. Museum of Mankind, London.

43

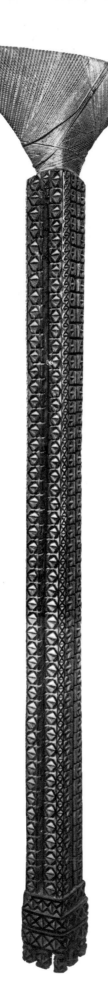

was driven towards Hawaii by a flood. Others say that she simply longed to travel and, tucking her little sister Hi'iaka (who had been born in the shape of an egg) under her arm, she set off. The story of her journey is told in a great Hula song, recorded by N. B. Emerson.

From Kahiki came the woman Pele,
From the land of Pola-Pola
From the red cloud of Kane,
Cloud blazing in the heavens,
Fiery cloud-pile in Kahiki.

Eager desire for Hawaii seized the woman Pele:

she carved the canoe, Honua-ia-kea,
Your canoe, O Ka moho alii,
They hasten the work on the craft to
*   completion,*
The lashings of the god's canoe are
*   done,*
The canoe of Kane, the world-
*   maker.*

Pola Pola, or Borabora, is an island in the Society group. Kamohoali'i was Pele's brother, and Honua-ia-kea means White Earth. Pele-of-the-sacred-earth acted as steerswoman and her travelling companions were the great gods Ku and Lono, as well as a host of little gods. Their arrival in the northern islands was heralded by eruptions and lightning flashes. Pele travelled from island to island searching for a place to live but every time she dug into the ground the sea poured in and drove her out. At last she burrowed into the great volcano Kilauea on the island of Hawaii, without striking water in the solid rock, and there she stayed.

The violent Pele did not improve her ways in her new home and soon even her faithful sister Hi'iaka was to suffer at her hands. One night while in a trance, Pele's spirit left her body

and, following the sound of a nose flute, arrived at a hula dance on a neighbouring island. Taking the form of a beautiful woman, she courted the young chief Lohiau. After three days she told him she had to leave but promised to send a messenger for him. On returning home Pele decided that only her faithful sister Hi'iaka could be entrusted with such a mission. She gave her sister super-natural powers to help her overcome any obstacles that she might encounter, and promised to look after her friend Hopoe and her groves of red and white flowering lehua trees.

The first hazard Hi'iaka met was the lizard-like mo'o monsters who tried to bar her way in the form of fog and sharp rain but she entangled them in a fast-growing vine. Her own powerful magic enabled her to detect others' tricks and when a monster made a false bridge of its tongue to lure the travellers to destruction, Hi'iaka saved her party by using her skirt as a bridge. At last she arrived at Lohiau's home only to find he had died of longing for the mysterious woman he had met at the hula dance. Hi'iaka caught his fluttering spirit and restored it to his body.

On their return journey Hi'iaka and Lohiau were delayed by the various spirits who opposed the match between Pele and a mere mortal. Meanwhile Pele began to regret having sent her attractive little sister to fetch her lover and her jealous imaginings reached such a pitch that she belched forth her lava streams, engulfing her sister's friend, Hopoe, and destroying the beautiful lehua blossoms.

The loyal Hi'iaka's own magic, however, enabled her to know of her sister's betrayal and as she journeyed her mood of bitterness and despair

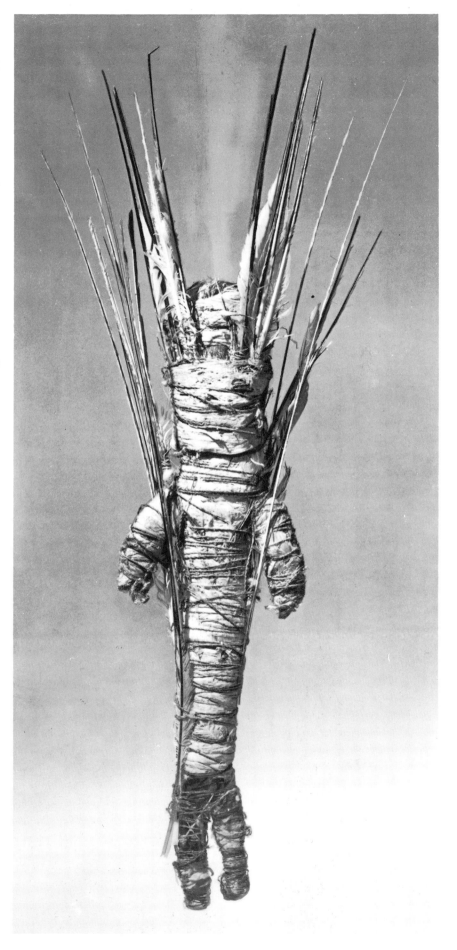

was reflected in the weather. N. B. Emerson has translated her song:

'Twas in Koolau I met the rain:
It came with a lifting and tossing of
*   dust,*
advancing in columns, dashing
*   along.*
The rain, it sighs in the forest;
The rain, it beats and whelms like
*   the surf;*
It smites, it smites now the land.
Pasty the earth from the stamping of
*   the rain;*
Full run the streams, a rushing flood;
The mountain walls leap with the
*   rain.*
See the water chafing its bounds like
*   a dog,*
A raging dog, gnawing its way to
*   pass out.*

Hi'iaka and Lohiau had one more adventure before they reached Pele's volcano. They were entertained by a prophetess called Pele-ula, who was no doubt Pele in another form. Hi'iaka contended with her hostess for the possession of Lohiau in a game of kilu. This game, which was a form of courtship, was played like quoits. A stake was placed in front of the desired one and the aim was to hit it with a spinning gourd. Although Hi'iaka won and Lohiau, in his turn, declared his love for her, she still refused to deceive her sister. She delivered him to the very brink of Pele's pit and there, overcome with grief and hysteria at the sight of her smoking and blackened groves, she embraced him. The enraged Pele encircled the lovers with her flames and consumed Lohiau, but Hi'iaka was protected by her own super-natural powers. Again she sought Lohiau's spirit and returned it to his body and together they returned to his own district.

Pele was hardly known outside the Hawaiian Islands. In Rarotonga there was Pere, a daughter of Mahu-ike, the goddess of fire who lived underground. The Maoris spoke of Parewhenua-mea, meaning the destructive force of a deluge. In Hawaii where the deluge occurred all too frequently in the form of an overwhelming lava flow, it is not surprising that Pele became a very important local deity. She provides the outstanding example in all Polynesia of the localisation and development of a character and the elaboration of incident to fill particular needs. Although her actual worshippers were limited to those who claimed her as an ancestor, many altars were erected to her beside lava streams. She also had her own priests. Both she and her sister were patronesses, not only of the hula but also of sorcery, and the great Pele-Hi'iaka story has been interpreted as a struggle between two rival schools of sorcery.

There are many stories about Pele and other members of her large family, but some of the most popular tell how Kamapua'a, the Hog-man, courted her. Kamapua'a had the power to transform himself into a plant or a fish as well as into a pig. In his human form he wore a cloak to hide the bristles down his back. When he wooed Pele she scorned him as a 'pig and a son of a pig'. Their taunts led to open combat. She almost overwhelmed him with fire and he retaliated by dousing her fires with fog and rain and over-running her districts with hogs. When only the sacred fire-sticks were left alight the gods intervened to restore the fires and Pele yielded to Kamapua'a. They divided the districts and Pele took Puna, Kau, and Kona where lava flowed while the Hog-man took Hilo and the other windward districts where it was always rainy, damp and moist.

Dr. Martha Beckwith, the great authority on Hawaiian mythology who retells the story, sees Kamapua'a as one aspect of the god of agriculture and as such he would be the natural rival of Pele the consumer of vegetation.

The Origin of Plant Foods and Things of Value

When the Polynesians' forbears spread across the Pacific they carried in their canoes most of the staple plant foods: root vegetables like the taro, yam and sweet potato, and shoots to propagate the breadfruit, banana, plantain and sugar cane; even the coconut was more likely to have been introduced to most islands by man rather than to have been carried by the sea. The climate and soil of atolls were often unsuitable for breadfruit, bananas and yams and the diet of the inhabitants was therefore limited. The islands were often places of famine, especially as population increased, and it is little wonder that some myths attributed famine to the withdrawal of foods by the gods, while others claimed that man had to steal what the gods enjoyed. Sometimes, however, new food was the gift of a god or a dead ancestor, or grew from part of the buried body of a god or mythological being. Food could also be the offspring of a deity.

Kepelino's *Traditions of Hawaii* recorded that Makali'i, a famous navigator, brought from Kahiki bananas, yams, sugar cane, arrow-root and gourds for making bottles and food containers. He had obtained these by tricking the inhabitants into exchanging these foods for 'new foods' which were actually branches of coral. Instead of sharing his loot when he returned to Hawaii, he kept it drawn up in a net, out of reach. His mean intentions were defeated by the cunning rat who gnawed the rope, broadcasting the plants over the land. The Hawaiians illustrated this tale with a figure which they made in string, showing the eight compartments of the net, each of which held one kind of vegetable. When the cord was cut where the rat was supposed to have nibbled the whole figure came apart.

Another Hawaiian story told how Kaulu tricked the gods into giving up cultivated foods. Kaulu was born in the shape of a rope and he had two brothers, one evil and one good. To keep Kaulu safe, his good brother placed him on a high shelf out of reach of the evil one until he matured into human shape. The fabulous feats he performed included breaking 'strong waves' into the large and small waves of the surf, and breaking a huge dog into a number of smaller dogs. He drained the sea to rescue his

Above J. Webber's drawing of the Boxing Match performed before Captain Cook, depicts the games during the *makahiki* festival in Hawaii when the god Lono, in the form of a pole with crossbar and bark cloth strips (*see* left) was carried round the island. Bernice P. Bishop Museum, Honolulu.

Opposite A carved wooden figure from Aitutaki in the Cook Islands. Staatliches Museum für Völkerkunde, Munich.

47

Fortunately saved the day by eating the fruit, the branches and the tree itself. Angry Hikuleo, goddess of the underworld, finally drove them out, but not before they had stolen yams and taro for man.

A common Polynesian motif is that of the all-providing and/or talking tree. Another Tongan tale, which incorporated this motif, was about a man called Longapoa who went on a journey with his chief. They voyaged through the red sea, the pumice sea, and the white sea, and were heading for the great whirlpool which led to the underworld when the horrified Longapoa managed to jump to safety. He was cast up on an island where a puko tree stood. When he wept from hunger the tree told him to prepare an oven, break off a branch and cook it. When he opened the oven he found pigs, yams and all sorts of good food. He was told he could take a branch of the tree home with him, but he was warned to plant it the moment he arrived. On reaching home, Longapoa was so overjoyed to see his family that he greeted them before he remembered to plant the branch. That is why the puko tree no longer produces food.

On Easter Island Alfred Métraux recorded a story of an old man nearing death who told his son that after eight days he would see a tree with its roots and branches floating in the sea. After the funeral rites the boy went to the shore and saw men already busy with a stranded tree. He cried out indignantly to them that it was his, but the men only teased him. So the boy addressed the tree, 'Old Man! Go! Stand up!' Immediately the tree began to float away over the horizon. The relatives of the boy begged him to call back the tree, for wood was a very precious commodity. The boy relented and called to the tree which floated ashore. The boy and his relatives cut branches '. . . to make statues, dancing paddles, lizards, paddles and clubs for killing people'.

Amongst the Maoris the planting and cultivation of the *kumara* (sweet potato) was accompanied by considerable ritual which culminated

brother who had been swallowed by the king of sharks, and spat it out again, thus making it salt. He flew up to the gods' vegetable patch in the heavens, and in the guise of a weakling, pestered the guards until they told him to take away what he could carry. At once he set to work and gathered up all there was and the gods had to beg him for a piece of each food to restock the garden.

The Tongans told to E. W. Gifford a similar story of trickery about five beings who visited the underworld of Pulotu. Although they hid themselves so successfully that they could not be seen, their smell betrayed their presence. At length they were flattered by the gods into showing themselves and then forced to undertake a series of tests. They were bidden to drink kava from a bowl as large as the sea. One of their number, called Perform Fortunately, not only did this but ate the bowl and the fibre strainers as well. Slippery Eel won the surfing contest and Stone won the diving contest. Octopus succeeded in plucking all the fruit from the tree without letting any fall and Perform

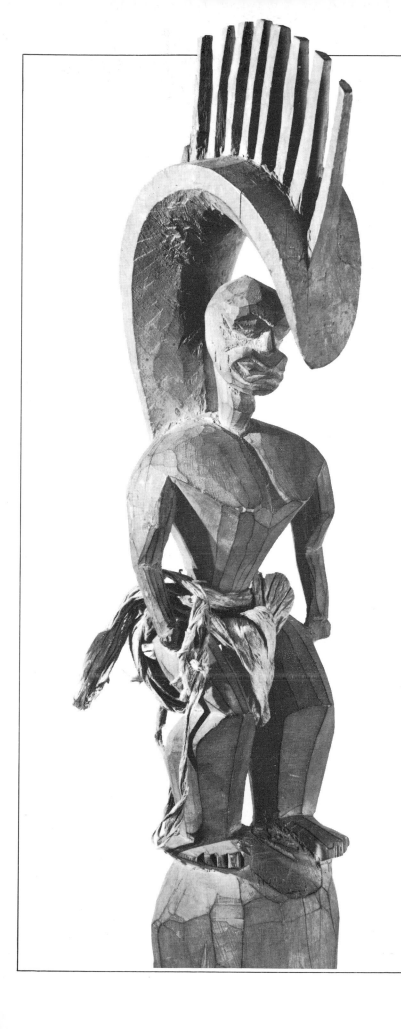

in the lifting of the crop by the priest when the appearance of the star called Whanui gave the signal for the harvest to begin. In the explanatory myth, Rongo-maui went to heaven to steal kumara from his brother Whanui. Concealing it in his loin-cloth, he returned to earth and impregnated his wife Pani. She went to the stream and gave birth to kumara in the water. One day she was disturbed by her sons and fled to the underworld where she continued to cultivate the kumara patch.

Similar stories about the first breadfruit are told on several islands. The Hawaiians say that a man called Ulu died during a famine and his body was buried near a spring. During the night his family could hear the sound of dropping leaves and flowers and then heavy fruit. In the morning they found a breadfruit tree growing from his grave and the famine was ended.

The coconut tree is a great provider. The young leaves can be plaited into baskets, hats and fans; the husks used to make sennit for caulking canoes and for making ropes and mats. The scooped out dry shells make containers and cups. The flesh can be eaten, the milk drunk and the oil rubbed on the body. Even a broken skull was mended with a piece of coconut shell. It is not surprising then to find that the myth of Hina and her eel lover, from whose buried head grew the first coconut tree, is told everywhere in Polynesia except Hawaii. Even in Easter Island, where there are neither coconuts nor eels, a remnant of the story was remembered.

A spirited though cryptic Tongan *solo* sung at a Kava ceremony tells the story of Hina, a protected virgin of high birth, living in Samoa, who was seduced by an eel while bathing in a pool; the angry people destroyed him.

The chant is from E. W. Gifford's *Tongan Myths and Tales* and it was quickened after the first four lines, when the drumming increased. Kaloafu and Teuhie named in the opening line were the eel's foster-parents.

49

Kaloafu and Teuhie
It is said had a pet child,
But it was a god,
Fled they madly because of their fear.
    Beat quickly!
They fled into the foaming sea.
The eel went to Samoa
And lived in Hina's water of life;
By and by Hina became pregnant.
'Oh Hina! Tell me who is your man?'
'It is the eel, the Shining One,'
Came all Samoa and cleaned,
And bailed the pool till it was empty;
Lifted out the eel and cut it to pieces,
Cut up and ate while Hina wept,
'Bring here the head to me,
Then bury it in the burying place.'
Nights five passed and then it
    appeared:
First came the leaf pod and fibre;
It was wonderful the way it grew;
And the coconut with light husks
Were heavy with oil for their child.
Cut down its body for a sun shelter.

Farther east the story of Hina and her eel lover, Tuna, was often incorporated in the Maui cycle. The Tahitians tell how Maui slew the eel and gave Hina the head to take home and plant, telling her that it contained great treasure for her. But foolish Hina left her bundle on the bank of a stream while she bathed. Too late she rememered Maui's instructions. She hurried from the water but the head had taken root and was already sprouting into a young coconut tree.

The Tuamotuans thought of Hina as a most experienced woman and included her story amongst those told to J. F. Stimson. Known as Hina-famed-in-story, she was both the daughter and the wife of Tiki. When he became ill she failed to revive him with her magic, thus bringing death to mankind. Next she became the mistress of Tuna-of-the-eternal-waters. Tiring of him she sought another lover but nobody wanted her because they were afraid of Tuna. At last Maui carried her off and Tuna came in pursuit, 'speeding over the combers of the ocean'. The rivals agreed to fight.

Tuna called on three great billowing waves 'to pile up, and up, until they towered above the land'.

The first broke over Maui and left him standing as if nothing had happened. The second broke over him as he crouched, clinging to a sacred coral slab from his temple, then 'he burst up through the welter of water' unharmed. Tuna came riding in on the third breaker with his mouth open ready to devour his rival, but Maui guessed his intentions and sent his coral slab riding before the wave straight for the beach. Tuna rode swiftly after it and as he seized the slab the sea receded leaving him stranded on dry land, at Maui's mercy. The hero cut him to pieces, and gave the monster's head to his mother, who planted it. There a coconut tree grew.

Two-faced Tinirau

Tinirau's realm was the ocean; he commanded the fish and used the shark and the whale as his messengers; he restocked the ocean with spawn from his fish-ponds; and from this activity came his name meaning 'myriad' or 'infinite'. He had two bodies, one divine and fish-like, and the other human, two faces and a dual personality.

In his human form Tinirau was handsome, charming – the man of every Polynesian girl's dream. He was the romantic hero of innumerable tales in which the heroine was a girl called Hina. She was characterised as an adolescent whose longings for the attentions of a lover and the independence of married status were tinged with fear of the unknown handsome stranger. Depending on where this

story was told he was called Tinirau, Sinilau, Kinilau, Timirau or Tinilau and she was called Hina, Hine, Sina or Ina.

In Eastern Polynesia Tinirau was called Lord of the Ocean and Engulfer. In this form he was truly fearful. He cast his shadow over the ocean in the shape of the hovering man-of-war bird and was visible in the white crests of the sullen Pacific rollers. Nobody knew when he would strike and he swallowed people by the canoe-load.

In western Polynesia Tinirau's place in the pantheon was ignored. He was simply a chief, or in the Samoan Islands a *manaia*, leader of young men. For this he did not even have to be high-born but could have attained this position of wealth and influence by his own natural abilities and qualities of leadership. Either way he was undoubtedly a most eligible bachelor. Hina was described as a high-born maiden, kept in seclusion. In Samoa such a girl was called a *taupou* and had many important ceremonial duties. Tinirau was usually one of many suitors who came to court her. Sometimes he even dared to break into her quarters, but the girl rejected him. Angrily he returned home, only to be pursued by Hina who had undergone a change of heart.

In eastern Polynesia her reasons for going in search of the mysterious Tinirau were more often a wish to escape tiresome parental restrictions or even punishment for neglecting household duties, or to avoid marrying someone she disliked.

Always Tinirau lived at a distance

Above Maori stone figure, referred to as a *kumara* (sweet potato) god, presumably because such figures have been dug up in the fields. Wanganui Museum.

Opposite A carved wooden figure from Tahiti. These figures were not representations of the gods; they were used by sorcerers who had the power to summon the spirit to enter the image. British Museum.

from Hina. In eastern Polynesia his home was a floating island, the Sacred Isle, Motu-tapu. In western Polynesia the Tongans said he lived in Samoa and the Samoans said he lived on the Tongan island of Vavau. The main incident of the plot always concerned Hina's plunge into the sea to find Tinirau's island, either by swimming or by riding on the backs of his sea creatures.

The Mangaians of the Cook Islands told W. W. Gill of Ina's journey in a song which concisely dramatises the highlights of her adventures.

Like a solitary tree is Ina
Who committed herself to the winds.
Ina invoked the aid of many fish
To bear her gaily on their backs;
The lordly shark to convey her safely
To the royal Tinirau o'er the sea.
Alas the bruised head of the angry
  monster,
who hitherto had obeyed the trem-
  bling maid,
who opened a coconut
On her voyage to the Sacred Isle.
Softly she beats the drum.
Tinirau is enchanted
By the music of the lovely one.

In more detail they explained that the 'many fish' Ina summoned were small, and finding her too heavy they tipped her into the shallow lagoon. After four attempts she had only reached the outer reef and her bearers had been permanently marked by her beatings. Next the sea-going shark agreed to carry her on his back. Halfway to the Sacred Isle she felt thirsty and the shark raised his dorsal fin so that she could pierce one of the coconuts she was carrying. After a time she was again thirsty and the shark raised his head. Ina gave it such a nasty crack with her coconut that she raised a lump which has ever since been called 'Ina's bump'. At once the shark shook her off and dived to the depths, leaving the girl to swim as best she could. Tekea the Great, the king of sharks, rose up to carry her, and protecting her from the attacks of other sharks, finally set her down on the beach of Tinirau's island.

As she came ashore the girl was astonished to see Tinirau's salt-water ponds, full of all kinds of fish. She came to his house but found it empty. Gently she beat on the great wooden drum which was standing in the room. The sweet notes filled the whole land and were heard by Tinirau in No-land-at-all, where he was staying. He quickly returned home, but Ina had hidden herself. He could find nobody and, mystified, set off again. But Ina had seen how handsome he was so she stood waiting for him when he returned.

The Mangaians described Ina and Tinirau's life together as a happy one. After a while she had a son and a daughter. One day her faithful brother Rupe visited her in the form of a pigeon. He brought about a reconciliation with her parents so that in later years she and her husband travelled between Mangaia and the Sacred Isle. But this happy ending is not typical of most versions. Particularly in the west, the story of their married life was embroidered with domestic details. As time passed she was neglected and even ill-treated by Tinirau. She was cast into the bush or even a pig-pen to bear her first child. Sometimes his other wives were blamed for turning him against her, or Tinirau himself excused his conduct by saying she was an unknown waif cast up by the sea, without name, family or dowry. When Rupe came to the rescue he established her status by opening his wings and showering the ground with gifts of great value. Then he carried off his sister and sometimes her son to his own country. In other accounts Tinirau kept the boy, but almost always there was another episode in which the parents were reconciled by their child.

This treatment of Hina was perhaps no more than a dramatisation of the typical feelings of a young wife, experiencing the pressures of a polygamous household, and homesick for her own people. The arrival of her brother Rupe to rescue her seems a fantasy-fulfilment of her longings to escape.

All this emphasis on domestic details masks the allegorical quality of the central theme: Hina's conscious choice of a husband who is the Engulfer or Death. In the story as told by the Maoris this was made explicit. Hina-uri deliberately attempted to drown herself. After some time she was thrown up on a beach, and although her body was overgrown with seaweed and barnacles, some traces of her beauty were still visible to her rescuers.

After further adventures Tinirau married her. In all these versions Hina seemed to acquire, by her sea-change, the ability to pass between the spirit world and the world of men, underlining the Polynesian belief in the co-existence of the supernatural and the natural.

Kae and Tinirau's whale

Another popular incident, the destruction of Tinirau's pet whale by Kae, was often a sequel to the story of Tinirau and Hina. The Maoris say that Tinirau summoned a priest called Kae to conduct the naming ceremony for their son. To honour him Tinirau cut a choice steak from the body of his pet whale, Tutunui. Unfortunately this gave the old priest a taste for the delicacy and he begged his host to lend him Tutunui to carry him home. Tinirau agreed but told Kae that when the whale got into shallow water he would shake himself as a sign for Kae to dismount and wade ashore, otherwise Tutunui would get sand in his blowhole and die. But the wicked Kae had other plans and as soon as he arrived home the whale was dragged from the water, killed, cooked and eaten. The savoury scent floated over the sea to Tinirau who sent a troupe of 40 dancing girls to investigate. He told them that they would recognise Kae by his crooked teeth.

The girls performed dances and sang funny songs that made everybody laugh and show their teeth; but the suspicious Kae kept his mouth tightly shut. At last he too laughed, revealing pieces of the whale's flesh sticking between his crooked teeth. That night the troupe threw everybody into an enchanted sleep, and arranging themselves in a long row from house to shore, they gently

passed the sleeping Kae down into the waiting canoe and bore him swiftly back to Tinirau, where he was killed and eaten. Some say that this was the origin of cannibalism.

Kae and the Island of Women

On the Marquesan island of Atuona the story of Kae was linked with the quite different but equally popular motif of the Island of Women. It has been recorded by E. S. C. Handy. Kae was cast up on the shores of a place where there were no men at all and all the women's husbands were pandanas roots. He married the chieftainess, Hina, and they had a son. After a while he became discontented and homesick because he discovered that while he grew older his wife, who had supernatural powers, regained her youth by surfing. She rode three times on the waves and the third time was carried onto the beach 'as fresh as a shrimp with its shell removed'. He insisted that he must return home to prepare the customary ceremonies for their child, who remained with her. So Hina lent him her brother the whale, Tunua-nui, to carry him. Of course Kae failed to obey her instructions to turn the whale round and people seized the animal, killed it and ate it. Kae told them to prepare a house, garden and pool for his son.

Meanwhile, the boy's playmates took to mocking him because he was the son of a stranger. He ran weeping to his mother, who at first denied he had a father and then promised to send him on the back of another great fish to his father's country. On arriving at Kae's island the obedient child turned the creature round so that he was facing towards home. But the people saw the fish, and believing it to be stranded, seized its tail to pull it ashore. Instead they were dragged into the sea and drowned. Thus the death of Tunau-nui was avenged.

The boy walked inland and bathed in the consecrated pool, ate the pigs and uprooted the garden. He was seized and was about to be killed for his impudence when he saved himself by reciting his name chant and his family genealogy. Kae recognised him and accepted him as his son.

Wonder-workers and Tricksters

Some of the most popular stories of Polynesia centred on characters who possessed extraordinary powers which derived from a supernatural source. They were both wonder-workers and mischief-makers or tricksters. The Hawaiians called them *kupua* and delighted in their adventures. They were born in non-human form, either as an egg which developed into a monstrous creature, or as a plant or inanimate object. They were usually brought up by their maternal grandparents who later supported them in their adventures with their magic. When they took human shape their supernormal nature was apparent in their ability to transform themselves, stretch or shrink themselves, fly through the air, take giant strides over the land and perform great feats of strength. Tales about them are concerned with how they slew monsters, rescued maidens, defeated rivals and even disputed with the gods in all sorts of games of skill, riddling competitions and trials of strength. Much of the humour of these stories depends on word-play and exaggeration.

There was Kawelo of Hawaii, a champion spear-thrower and expert fisherman who was almost defeated in battle when his opponent shamed him by calling him 'son of a cock' – a pun on his name. He saved himself by retorting, 'The cock roosts above the chief, the cock is chief.' Another Hawaiian favourite was Pekoi, the rat-shooter who strung forty rats by their whiskers with one arrow.

Iwa, a master thief, was a great trickster 'who stole while he was yet in his mother's womb'. He had a magic paddle which carried him in four strokes from one end of the Hawaiian chain to the other. In a famous contest with six other professionals, in which each had to fill a house completely with stolen goods in a single night, he waited until the others had filled their houses and gone to sleep and then he stole everything from theirs to fill his own.

The Marquesans told about fabulous Ono, born as an egg and brought up on air by his grandfathers. He was a great fisherman, wrestler and powerful magician. When he was killed he reconstituted himself and displayed even more terrifying magic by alternately stretching himself up to the sky and becoming small again. Then he broke himself into pieces and suddenly became whole again.

The most famous stretching *kupua* of Hawaii was Kana, who was born in the form of a rope and brought up by his grandmother, Uli. He was asked to rescue a woman who had been abducted and placed on an island-hill. Each time Kana tried to reach her by growing taller the hill grew taller too, lifting the girl further away. Soon he became as thin as a cobweb and very hungry, so he bent over to Hawaii and put his head through his grandmother's door, where she fed him. She also told him that the island was really a turtle whose stretching power lay in his flippers. Kana broke these off and rescued the girl. David Malo has recorded a prayer in which jugglers appealed to Kana:

Put on your rope body,
Lay off your human form
In this trick of yours and mine, O
    Kana.

Maui, Challenger of the Gods

Maui was, without doubt, the greatest Polynesian trickster. Not only did he slay monsters, rescue maidens, defeat rivals like Tuna the eel, and recover his wife from the eight-eyed Bat, he deliberately challenged the authority of the gods in order to make the world a more pleasant place for men. Abandoned at birth by his mortal mother because

Opposite Maori meeting-house panel depicts Maui's fishing exploits. Museum für Völkerkunde, Hamburg.

Above Marquesan carved stilt foot-rests.
Stilt walking was a sport indulged in on
ceremonial occasions, when men would
race for wages. Women were forbidden
to participate. Museum of Mankind,
London.

Opposite A Maori kite in the form of a bird
with a human head. The wings span six
feet (two metres). Kite-flying has many
mythological associations in Polynesia.
The Maoris say Tawhaki ascended to the
sky world as a kite or by means of a kite.
One version says his wings were broken
when he fell and another says he

abandoned his kite for a hawk. The Maoris
of Chatham Island have charms called
Tawhakis which they recite to disperse
storms. These refer to Tawhaki as a kite,
and Rata has similar associations.
Museum of Mankind, London.

of his premature state, and carried off
either by his divine father or grandparents, he grew into an ugly but
intelligent little boy who rapidly
learnt all that the gods could teach
him. Although he was brought up by
the gods he chose to identify himself
with men. Most narrators place him
in the fourth generation after the
primeval pair, Atea and Papa, when
there was still much to do in the
world; the sky pressed down on the
earth and disorder prevailed; the sun
travelled too quickly and the days
were too short to cook, make tapa, or
build houses and canoes; many useful
skills were as yet unknown. Maui set
out to rectify this state of affairs with
considerable enthusiasm and sometimes near-disastrous repercussions.
He helped to raise the skies; he fished
up lands, stole fire, snared the sun,
controlled the winds and arranged the
stars. Not that his contemporaries
were all that appreciative of his
achievements, for they feared him and
were envious of his powers. They
mocked him for his irregular birth,
strange appearance and uncouth
ways. Even at his most heroic there
was something of a buffoon about
him. Moreover he dissipated his
energes in acts of meanness like the
transformation of his brother-in-law
into a dog. In the end men found his
behaviour embarrassing and the gods
considered him troublesome. Unlike
most other wonder-working heroes
who simply fade out of things, Maui's
career, according to some narrators,
was ended by death. In his last great
adventure he strove to achieve
immortality for man. His failure was
attributed to mortals who, tired of
his tricks, either deliberately betrayed
him or simply let him down.

He was called Maui-of-a-thousand-
tricks and Maui-tupua-tupua,
meaning super-super-man. Amongst
the Maoris he was known as Maui-
the-wise. In Tahiti his wisdom was
said to have come from his having
eight heads, for when his divine
fosterparents saw him they said,
'Nothing can escape that sort of man
– with eight heads! Look how reflec-
tive he is!'

Many Polynesians called him

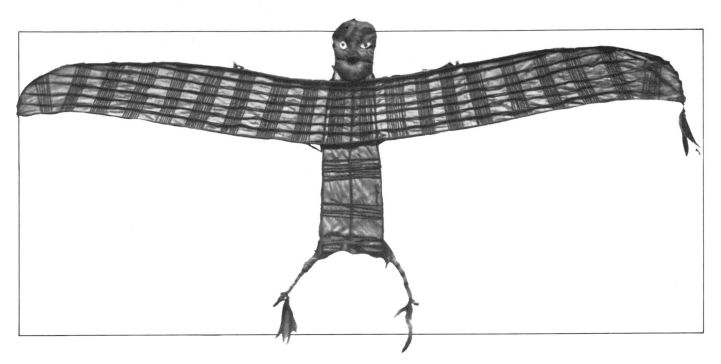

Maui-tikitiki-a-Taranga, a reference to his being cradled at birth by his mother, Taranga, in a topknot of her hair. Sometimes, as in Samoa, the epithet tikitiki-a-Taranga has survived where the proper name has been lost. Outside Polynesia his name is recognisable in a variety of Micronesian and Melanesian adaptations. Even in the Philippine Islands, amongst the Igorot tribe, there was a hero called Lumauig who resembled him. When his name was absent some of his deeds and adventures were often appropriated by local culture heroes and/or tricksters like Matuarang, son of Nareau, in Kiribati and Qat in the Banks Islands.

Maui has an outstanding biographer and analyst in the person of Dr. Katherine Luomala who, in her book *Maui-of-a-thousand-tricks*, demonstrated how different narrators rearranged episodes and subordinated incidents to give the cycle of stories about Maui a different emphasis in every group 'and yet how tenaciously certain deeds and names cling to the vast myth-complex associated with the name of Maui'. In Rarotonga where Maui was said to be the son of the god, Tangaroa, his actions were directed towards avenging his father who felt insulted when he was knocked over by the shark, Mokoroa, and all the other gods laughed. The Marquesan and

the Tuamotuan narratives were distinctly erotic in style. In Tonga there was much elaboration of monster-slaying incidents. In the Society Islands the trickster elements were subordinated and Maui became a pillar of the establishment; the motive for his snaring the sun being to give his brother Maui-mua, the priest, more time to build his temples. In the account collected by Sir George Grey from the Arawa tribe, New Zealand, the plot has been most skilfully re-organised to link the inevitability of Maui's death with his father's failure to use the proper ritual at his baptismal ceremony.

Tales about Maui are therefore especially interesting to students of comparative folklore because they provide an opportunity for the study of dispersal, persistence and elaboration of major mythological themes like sun-snaring, land-fishing, fire-stealing and sky-raising. They are also very rich in small details which recur in all sorts of stories throughout Oceania and which folklorists regard as the 'stock-in-trade' of Oceanic oral literature. Some common ones are the blocking of the chinks in a house to keep out the daylight, causing somebody to oversleep; lifting a tuft of grass which covers the entrance to the underworld; and a bird character who drops berries or seeds on somebody to attract attention.

The order in which Maui's feats were arranged in a cycle varied from island to island, but the exploit which probably received the most elaboration was his fishing up of lands. The Hawaiians said their islands were a shoal of fish belonging to Mr. One-Tooth, who lived under the sea. Maui sought the help of Hina-the-Bailer to draw them together as one piece of land. She fastened his magic hook in Mr. One-Tooth's mouth and as Maui hauled on the line, he ordered his brothers to row without looking back, but their curiosity got the better of them. When they disobeyed him, the islands broke away, the smaller ones flying like baby porpoises trying to keep up with their mother. Mr. One-Tooth finally tethered them in their present positions.

A robust rendering of the land-fishing episode comes from a narrator of Anaa in the Tuamotuan archipelago, translated by J. F. Stimson. There the deep-sea fishermen had to be skilful navigators to negotiate the dangerous reefs and waters of the group. Maui's brothers, fearing his tricks, were not very happy to have him join their fishing expedition. Their fears increased when he demanded that they paddle a long way out of sight of land before casting their lines. They fished but caught nothing. Exhausted, they decided to sleep. Before they dropped

Above Panel in the Maori meeting house, To Kanganui a Noho at Te Kuiti, which depicts Maui snaring the sun. (*See also* page 19.)

Opposite Figure from Easter Island, made of tapa cloth stretched over bound bullrushes and decorated with a tattoo pattern. Usually placed near the door of a house, it was believed to offer protection against evil spirits. Peabody Museum of Archaeology and Ethnology, Harvard University, Cambridge, Massachusetts.

off Maui said to ignore any noises and simply row straight for land when he woke them up. While they slept Maui cast his line and chanted to give power to his hook.

*Oh, the miraculous fishing feat of
  Maui!*
*The fish of Maui was hauled steadily
  upwards*
*And his belt-strap loosened and
  dropped off – oho!*
The illustrious fishing feat of Maui
*Oh, the illustrious fishing feat of
  Maui!*
*His girdle slipped down – it was
  called*
*Maro-takai-tahi, Girdle-of-a-single-
  turn,*
His foot flew up – oho!
The far-famed fishing feat of Maui –
*Oh, the far-famed fishing feat of
  Maui!*
His fish rose to the surface of the sea,
And rolled over – oho!
The mighty fishing feat of Maui!
Oh, the mighty fishing feat of Maui!
His fish broke up through the wave
Here in this world of light above!
*And his elder brothers cried, 'O
  Maui! This is not a fish –
  it is an island!'*
'So it is! Oho!'

At these words the line broke, the fish escaped. Maui fell back into the canoe 'weeping with vexation'.

Next time they went fishing he used his grandfather Mauike's hook, called Makinokino, the long-enduring, and his line Ruku-i-henua, attached-to-land. Again his elder brothers were angry when Maui insisted that they paddle far out to sea, and again he suggested they rest while he fished. He warned them: 'Do not interfere with me, no matter what happens.' He cast his line and chanted:

*It is the rope – a rope of rolled and
  twisted strands.*
Cast down into the sea – paid out.
*It is a rope of twirled and twisted
  strands flung down into the far
  depths below!*
*It is the rope – a noosed rope,
  destined to retrieve the land (from
  the dark abyss) –*
A possession of the God.

Once again Maui's great performance was marred by his foolish brothers. For as the great fish broke the surface his brothers woke up and again cried, 'O, Maui! O, Maui! that's not a fish, it's an island!' The fish thrashed about and the body broke at the head end. But some of it held fast to Maui's rope. He had fished up Havaiki and he and his family went to live there.

Maui's relationship with his brothers and his parents is worked out most completely in the Arawa version. Maui was born prematurely and his mother wrapped him in a tuft of her hair and threw him into the foam of the surf. Her prayers saved him from becoming a malicious spirit, the usual fate of an aborted or premature foetus. The seaweed formed and fashioned him and soft jellyfish protected him until his great ancestor, Tama of the Sky, found him and hung him up in the rafters, where he was revived by the warmth of the fire.

One night the little Maui decided to leave his fosterparent and go in search of his real family. He found them at a dance in the Great Assembly House. He sat behind one of his brothers so that when the time came to go home and his mother counted her children on her fingers, she came to a fifth child who said, 'I am your child too!'

She denied this was possible until Maui convinced her by telling her the story of his birth. Then she took him and cuddled him in preference to his brothers who became jealous and spoke of him as 'a little abortion' who has 'the impudence to call himself a relation of ours'.

Each day the mother disappeared at dawn and Maui resolved to find out where she went. The little fellow hid her clothes and blocked up all the chinks that let in the light, so that she overslept. When at last she woke up and rushed off crying, he saw her snatch up a tuft of rushes and disappear underground. To the delight of his brothers, Maui transformed himself into a pigeon. His mother's white tapa belt, which he had stolen, became beautiful white breast feathers. Then he too lifted the tuft

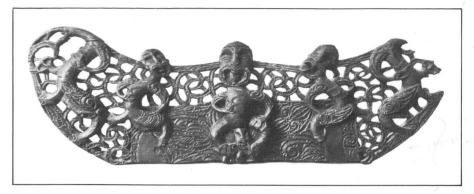

Left Carved door lintel of a Maori meeting house, now in Wanganui Museum, said to depict Maui being destroyed by Hina – crushed between her thighs – as he tried to enter her and gain immortality for man.

Opposite A carved wooden image from Hale-o-Keawe, the mausoleum of the house of Keawe at Honaunau. (*See* page 23.) Pitt Rivers Museum, Oxford.

and flew underground, dipping his wings because the cave was so narrow. At last he came to a garden where his parents were working. He perched in a tree above them and dropped berries on them until his father tried to catch him, then he turned back into human form. His mother told his father who he was and his father took him and performed the baptismal ceremony. Unfortunately he accidentally left out a line in the ritual. At once he realised that the consequence of his error would be Maui's death.

Maui now began to use his magic to further his exploits; but he wanted to increase his power so he starved his old grandmother to death to obtain her enchanted jaw-bone. Next he snared the sun in a noose of native flax as it rose from its pit below the horizon. Using the enchanted jaw-bone as a weapon, he beat the sun to make it go more slowly so that people would have more time to tend their gardens.

Elsewhere in Polynesia the most common reason given for slowing down the sun was to allow more time for cooking because people's mouths were sore from eating raw food. In Hawaii, the Marquesas and Samoa it was said that Maui wanted to give his mother, or his wife, more time to make tapa cloth. In many accounts the rope which Maui used to bind the sun were hairs from his mother's sacred head.

In the Arawa version Maui's land drawing hook was also fashioned from his grandmother's enchanted jaw-bone, and he drew blood from his own nose to use as bait. He left his catch in his brothers' care while he went to perform a thanksgiving ceremony. They disobeyed his instructions and began to cut up the fish before his return, making it jump and wriggle about. This caused the unevenness of the New Zealand landscape, and the Maoris also say that his hook became the southern headland of Hawke's Bay.

In spite of a warning from his mother not to anger his ancestress, Mahui-ike, keeper of fire in the underworld, Maui next strove to steal fire for mankind. He visited Mahui-ike and asked her for fire to light his cooking oven. The old lady plucked out one of her fingernails containing fire and gave it to him. He took it and extinguished it. Then he returned and begged for another, saying that the first one had gone out. He repeated this prank nineteen times until Mahui-ike had only one toenail left. Only then did she realise that she was being tricked. Angrily she dashed the last nail on the ground, setting everything alight. Although Maui changed himself into an eagle to escape the flames his wings were singed brown. He called down the rain to put out the fire and Mahui-ike just managed to save a few sparks by throwing them into trees as she fled. Ever after man has made fire from the wood.

Maui's next prank, in the Arawa version, was quite a heartless one, that incidentally accounted for the origin of dogs. He changed his brother-in-law, Irawaru, into a dog and so upset his sister, Hina-uri, that she tried to drown herself. (This was the same Hina-uri who later married Tinirau.) The Tuamotuans allowed Maui some justification for his nasty trick. In their version they said Maui turned Ri, his wife's lover, into a dog, not out of jealousy but because he

was fed up with not getting his meals on time. The Arawa narrator, however, saw it as one more nail in Maui's coffin. For after this trick feeling against him was so strong that he had to return to his father's village.

His father, although he knew that Maui must die, goaded him to challenge the Great-goddess-of-the-night, Hine-nui-te-po, and seek immortality for man. He pointed to the distant flashing where the edge of the horizon met the sky, and told Maui that there he would find his ancestress. 'Her hair is like tangles of seaweed, her eyes are like red fire, her mouth like a barracouta's, her teeth as sharp as volcanic glass, and her body like that of a man.'

Maui set forth with only the small forest birds for company. When they arrived at Great Hina's dwelling they found her asleep. Maui explained to his friends how he intended to creep into Hina's body and emerge again from her mouth. Above all, he warned them not to laugh until he reappeared or he would be killed. They watched anxiously while Maui threw off his garments, revealing his beautifully tattooed skin, mottled and gleaming like the scales of a mackerel, and disappeared between the thighs of the dreaded goddess until only his legs were visible. It was such a funny sight that the little birds screwed up their tiny cheeks, trying to suppress their laughter. At last the little wagtail could contain himself no longer and let one merry cheerful note escape. Hina woke and crushed Maui within her and ever since then all men die. The Maori proverb says: 'Men make heirs, but death carries them off'.

Only in New Zealand was the theme treated with such grandeur. In

the Tuamotus Maui attempted to achieve immortality by exchanging his intestines with those of a sea slug, but gave up when his brothers expressed their disgust.

Though Maui was not worshipped as a god, many chants, spells and invocations first used by him to assist him in his mighty feats were repeated by his many admirers to strengthen their own actions. His stories were not part of sacred lore – they belonged to everybody. His great popularity undoubtedly derived from delight in his prowess and sympathy for his weaknesses. In a society dominated by the concept of tapu, the common people always enjoyed and got emotional release from seeing the righteous, the stuffy and the superior discomfited.

With the coming of Christianity the Polynesians abandoned their own gods but the tremendous popularity of Maui ensured his survival. Just as he had adapted himself to many different circumstances on many different islands in the past, so he did again. Some Hawaiians, on hearing about Jesus Christ, likened him to Maui years before the Freudian psychologist, Otto Rank, made similar comparisons. Polynesian preachers used stories about Maui to illustrate their sermons, and Dr. Peter Buck (Te Rangi Hiroa), as part of a filibuster in the New Zealand parliament in support of a Bill to introduce daylight-saving, told how Maui snared the sun.

The Westward Journey of the Soul

Maui failed to obtain immortality for man and ever since then men's souls have departed from their bodies after death and taken the pathway to the leaping place which exists on every island. The Maoris took the road to Reinga at the northern-most point of the North Island and there descended into a nether world by a long pendant root. On most other islands the leaping place faced west and associated with it was a special tree. The Hawaiians called it a 'quietly calling

61

Above Engraving after J. Webber's drawing of a Hawaiian chief made on Cook's third voyage. The crested helmet and feather cloak were worn by men of rank.

Opposite The delicately carved handle of a fly-whisk, formerly attributed to the Society Islands, now regarded as of Austral Islands type. Formerly Hooper Collection.

breadfruit tree' and said that the spirit of little children stayed nearby to direct the dead. In Mangaia the great tree which grew up from the underworld had one branch reserved for each clan on the island. A common Polynesian belief was that the tree had misleading branches; one side was dry and brittle and the other green. By grasping the dry branches the soul could save itself from falling into the depths of Po.

The soul's fate was either to return to the amorphous nothingness which was Po or to enter a spirit world which was called Pulotu in western Polynesia and Hawaiki in eastern Polynesia. Hawaiki was also the name given to the ancestral homeland in the west; a place with which the living had lost contact but to which the spirits could still return. It became therefore the desired destination of the soul after death. It was said to be located either on an island in the west, in the sky, under the sea or below ground. If it was thought of as an underworld it was often confusingly called Po.

Wherever these after-worlds were located they tended to be divided into several regions. One of these regions of Po was ruled by Miru (Milu) who, some islanders believed, waited below the leaping place with his net to catch the souls of the common people, wrongdoers, and those unfortunate enough to have been killed by sorcery. They were thrown into his ovens where they experienced unending death. In spite of the apparent similarity between Miru's fires and the eternal hellfire of Christians, the Polynesians did not believe in punishment or reward after death as a result of behaviour in this life. They were not tortured by Miru's fires; they were annihilated.

The privileged classes expected to join their ancestors in a spirit world which was a replica of this one, but the soul could not make such a journey unaided. It required the assistance of its relatives, both living and dead. Failure to carry out the proper funeral rites meant that a spirit might linger in this world and become malevolent or it might be condemned to a twilight zone to feed on moths and butterflies. It became imperative therefore to recover the physical remains of a parent or loved one who died in a strange country. This was the main motive for the journeys of two great Polynesian heroes, Tawhaki and Rata.

Guardian spirits, called *ammakua* by the Hawaiians, came to meet the soul and protect it from the perils of the journey. Sometimes they came in numbers to welcome the spirit of an important personage and many

Hawaiians claimed to have heard the chanting voices and high flute notes of the Marchers of the Night. It was said that if one actually met them the wisest thing to do was to remove all clothing and lie face upwards, feigning sleep.

Few mortals have ever visited these regions and returned. Those that have done so certainly required the assistance of their guardian spirits. Once they secured this however they could make the journey in many ways: by climbing a rainbow, or a hanging vine or aerial root, or by climbing a stretching tree. The Stretching Coconut Tree or the Far-travelling Coconut was a favourite symbolic link between a man and his ancestors in the spirit world. Sometimes a canoe chosen for such a journey was called Rainbow or Sheath of the Coconut.

The Maoris tell the story of Pare who at first encouraged the advances of Hutu and then refused him her favours. Angered by his rejection he left and the girl, overcome by shame, hanged herself and descended to Po. Hutu still longed for her, so with the assistance of Great Hina he followed her to the underworld. There he attempted to attract Pare's attention by practising all the sports she loved to watch, like top-spinning and spear-throwing. But she would not show herself. At last Hutu invented a new sport by bending down a tree and swinging up on it. Pare could not resist this and joined him. Together they swung higher and higher until Hutu was able to grasp the roots of the plants at the entrance to Po and climb with Pare into the world of light. He returned her soul to her body by forcing it through the soles of her feet.

In a similar story from Hawaii, the hero in search of his loved one rubbed his body with rancid oil to dull the human smell and avoid detection in the underworld. In the Marquesan story about Kena, whose mother's supernatural powers protected him on his journey to Havaiki under the sea to rescue his wife Tefio, emphasis was placed on the hazards of the journey. He survived encounters with ogres and sirens and at the entrance

to the fourth Havaiki he passed between clashing rocks where his companion, who was holding on to his loincloth, was crushed to death. He was allowed to carry Tefio's spirit back to the world in a basket, but he was warned not to release her for any reason for ten days. Alas, when night came, he could not resist opening the basket. Tefio's spirit jumped out and sped back to Havaiki. Kena made the journey a second time and once again recovered his beloved Tefio, but this time he obeyed the tapu.

The Noble Tawhaki, and Rata the Strong

Ordinary men are dragged down by their weaknesses but every so often there comes a man who shows how life should really be lived. On almost every island tales were told about two such men, the noble Tawhaki and Rata-the-unique, and in New Zealand, the Tuamotus, Rarotonga, Tahiti and Hawaii, their thrilling achievements mark the high points of a great cycle of myths which trace the fortunes of the same family through five successive generations.

The basic plot as told by the Maoris was that Whaitiri, a cannibal chieftainess, came from the sky to marry Kaitangata, whose name means 'man-eater', only to discover that this referred to his prowess as a fighter, not to his diet. After having two children, Hema and Punga, and going blind because of her evil ways, she returned to her own land. In another Maori variant the husband complained about the mess and smell of the children's excrement so, after inventing the latrine, the wife returned to her own country. In Hawaii the wife was Hina-who-worked-in-the-moon and she returned to the moon because she wearied of disposing of the children's mess.

The eldest child Hema grew up and married a goddess. They had two children Tawhaki and Kariki. While seeking a birth gift in foreign lands Hema trespassed on the territory of the goblins who seized him and gouged out his eyes to use as lights and then threw him into a latrine. The great central story of the cycle told of Tawhaki's journey to find his father and avenge him. He was accompanied by his brother Kariki whose clumsiness served as a foil to his dignity and skill. In his search for his father he found a wife (who was usually a goddess) and they had a child called Wahieroa who was, in his turn, fated to be captured (because he trespassed or broke a tapu) but not before he too had a son, Rata, who was also destined to sail in search of his father in a canoe fashioned by the spirits of the forest.

The cycle demonstrated the interdependence of successive generations, the conduct of each man being determined by that of his father before him. It also showed that the success of any action depended on the co-operation of the spirit world, particularly on the supernatural forces controlled by a man's maternal ancestors, for their power extended beyond the borders of his own land and was the kind of protection required on a quest or a journey of revenge.

In most versions Tawhaki's birth was preceded by predictions of his greatness. The Maoris called him a god of thunder and lightning, but mostly he was described as a chief. It was said that no man had such gleaming red skin as his, a true symbol of his god-like nature. The Tuamotuans claimed that the very sight of him made women distraught with love. The Mangarevans told how rivals turned themselves into fish and waited under the water to tear his skin off during a diving competition. His maternal grandmother guessed their plan and she too hid underwater and gathered the bits of skin into her basket. Although she stuck them all back on again, there were not quite sufficient to cover the soles of his feet because the stick insects had stolen some small pieces to make red patches under their arms.

Even as a child Tawhaki's nobility and generosity was evident — and aroused envy. The Tahitians said that his cousins, the children of Puna, could not abide the way his toy canoes won every race. They beat him until they thought they had killed him, and left him on the beach. The forbearing Tawhaki got up and followed them home and did not even complain to his mother. Much later, when the opportunity presented itself, he simply turned them into porpoises. It was from the obscene chants of these children that he learnt of his father's shameful fate and determined to rescue him. Some narratives say that he recovered his father's bones; others that he found him still alive, lifted him from the cess-pit, washed him clean and replaced his eyes. He also destroyed the goblins, to whom light was fatal, by closing all the chinks in the house so that they slept into the hours of daylight, and were trapped.

An episode commonly linked with Tawhaki was his encounter with his blind grandmother who guarded the way to the other world. Sometimes he met her in his search for his father, but one Maori narrator says that the encounter took place when he went to recover his wife, who had returned in a huff to her home in the sky. He found the old lady sitting near the end of the swinging vine that led to the heavens. She was counting out the ten taro roots she was about to cook. Tawhaki slipped them away, one by one, until she guessed somebody was tricking her. Angrily she swung her great fish hook trimmed with red feathers to catch the thief. (The Tuamotuans claimed that she succeeded in hooking Kariki and only let go when Tawhaki threatened to send the red shark to devour her.) Then Tawhaki touched her eyes and restored her sight. She at once recognised her grandchildren and agreed to help them to reach the heavens. Foolish Kariki did not heed her instructions and seized the loose stem of the vine which swung him to the very edge of the sky and back again – he was on his way to the other side when Tawhaki managed to arrest his flight and save him from destruction. He sent Kariki home and continued the journey alone. Taking the piece of vine which was firmly anchored to the ground, he climbed into the sky.

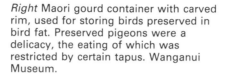

Opposite A Maori flute of the type known as *koauau.* Usually played by mouth, though some examples could be played as a nose flute. University Museum of Archaeology and Anthropology, Cambridge.

Right Maori gourd container with carved rim, used for storing birds preserved in bird fat. Preserved pigeons were a delicacy, the eating of which was restricted by certain tapus. Wanganui Museum.

The old blind grandmother whose sight was restored in return for her assistance is a popular Polynesian motif. It also occurs in stories about Maui or Tane. Sometimes her sight was restored by a slap, or an application of clay or spittle, or by throwing two young coconuts at her eyes. The presence of this element in some 'Swan Maiden' stories of Melanesia strengthens the similarity between the Swan Maiden theme and the recurring theme of the cycle, in which a girl came from the sky to marry a mortal but later returned because of a quarrel over a trivial matter; although the important element of compulsion – namely that the swan maiden was forced to stay because the man kept her wings – is missing.

It seems that men cannot learn from the mistakes of their forefathers and Wahieroa, son of Tawhaki, suffered the same fate as his grandfather Hema. The Tuamotuans say that Puna was angry because the water nymph, Tahiti Tokerau, deserted him for the mortal Wahieroa and that they fell into his power while fishing on the reef for crabs for their child, Rata. Matuku-tago-tago, the shark, bit off Wahieroa's head and carried off Tahiti Tokerau to Puna's dwelling. Her eyes were plucked out to serve as lights for her sister, who had become Puna's wife. Then she was thrust head first into the sand so

that her feet became supports for her sister's baskets.

As in the story of Tawhaki, Rata learnt the truth about his parents, not from his guardian Kui, but from children who chanted mockingly as they played with their toy boats. The translation is by J. F. Stimson:

Let your boat speed on ever so swiftly, O Rata!
Never shall your father be avenged –
Flung into the sea, swallowed by Matuku-tago-tago,
called Black-cloud-of-the-horizon!
And as for your mother – her legs swing to and fro in the winds
beside the latrine of the woman, Huarei!

Rata also determined to avenge his father, but he was quite unlike Tawhaki in personality. Although he was strong, courageous and persistent, he was also impetuous and thoughtless. The story of how Rata built his great double canoe and sailed to the Land of the Moonlight Border, is one of the truly great sagas of the Pacific. The Tuamotuans, themselves great sailors, delighted in singing of how Rata first antagonised the gods but later won their support because of the justice of his cause, and how they sailed with him on his voyage of revenge. In the story they told J. F. Stimson, Rata cut down the tree for his canoe with Kui's enchanted axe, Great Helve of

Hibiscus Wood, but he had chosen a tapu tree in the sacred valley and it was lifted up again by the wood sprites. When Rata saw this he chopped it down again and hid to see what would happen. The sprites returned, led by Tavaka, the Gouge and Togo-hiti, the stick insect, and began to chant:

Fly hither, fly hither the chips of my tree!
Right here to cling,
Right here to fall in place.

At these words the chips flew into place and then at a similar command, the sap, the bark, the leaves returned to the tree and it was raised upright. Rata was so angry that he quite forgot himself and shouted 'Pa-a-a-a!' in a great voice, causing the sprites to fall over themselves with fright. When Rata explained why he had presumed to cut the sacred tree they forgave him and, in one night, Tavaka and his band had built the canoe for him and delivered it to his door on a rainbow.

Rata set out on his journey with the wood sprites as an invisible crew. He exulted in the firm, fast ship under his feet and sang of Kui, who flew above him as a tropic bird, seeking out the 'pathway of the seas' and revealing the hidden places of Puna's sea demons so that Rata could destroy them. There was the great shark, Matuku, a swordfish, Devourer-of-Multitudes, and a giant clam. From the belly of the shark Rata recovered his father's head and from each of the other monsters he recovered other parts of his father's body. He gently laid them in a basket lined with the softest tapa cloth. As his ship neared Puna's land, the last obstacle, an enchanted reef, rose up to encircle and protect it. Rata broke through this with his enchanted axe.

His ship entered the lagoon while Puna slept, and he managed to divert the attention of the lizard guards. Then the rooster sentries gave the alarm but Rata was able to lasso his enemy before he was properly awake, and drag him aboard his canoe where he was promptly hacked to pieces. It only remained for him to rescue his mother and restore her sight.

So ended the story of Rata-the-Unique. No wonder that ruling Polynesian chiefs like King Pomare of the Society Islands and King Kalakaua of Hawaii were proud to claim this great voyager hero as their ancestor.

The Pattern of Polynesian Myth

In this account of Polynesian mythology the emphasis has been placed throughout on the homogeneity of mythological themes in spite of the separation of island groups from each other in both time and distance. But when the myths of only one group are considered sometimes a particular leitmotif emerges which seems to give expression to underlying social tensions. In those of the Marquesas Islands, for instance, a repeated theme is that of the man-devouring woman. In story after story men are captured by siren-like *vahine-hae* who can be recognised, if one catches them unawares, by their eyes which pop out, and tongues which flick down to the ground. Children are constantly being devoured by ogresses or deprived of food by a mother or a foster-mother who hides it in a hollow in her back.

These stories occurred in a society in which the households were polyandrous and there was apparently much male sexual frustration. Other strong frustrations stemmed from food scarcity.

Without making rash psychological generalisations it is worth noting that, fascinating though it is to follow the trail of one character, one incident, one theme, one story-detail, from island to island across the Pacific, it is equally illuminating to see how a particular culture takes these and makes them a unique expression of its own view of life.

Opposite A characteristically carved figure from the Marquesas – it was attached to the canoe prow through the holes in the base so that the projection extended over the water. Formerly Hooper Collection.

Micronesia

The Background

When Magellan visited Guam in 1521, the Chamorro, who were the indigenous population of the Mariana Islands, had the doubtful honour of being the first Oceanians to receive European callers. Although Guam continued to be a port of call for the Spaniards on their way to Manila, the first real attempt to assert Spain's suzerainty did not take place until 1668, when the Jesuits and soldiery set about converting and subduing the islanders. Several great typhoons at the end of the 17th century were nature's footnote to the carnage wrought by the Spaniards. By 1710 an estimated population of 100,000 had been reduced to little more than 3500. A few Chamorro escaped to the neighbouring Caroline Islands where they kept their identity as a people.

In the years that followed, the Mariana Islands north of Guam became completely depopulated. By the late 19th century, although the population of Guam had increased again, it had become a mixture of Chamorro, Filipino and Spanish stock. The aboriginal language had survived but the oral traditions had been swamped by introduced elements. Fragments only of recognisable Oceanic themes persisted in popular tales like that of the great fish which was said to be undermining the thin neck of land which separates Agana Bay from Pago Bay, until the Virgin Mary tethered it with one of her hairs and saved the island of Guam from destruction.

No other Micronesians suffered from the unwanted attentions of Europeans quite so rapidly or drasti-cally as the Chamorro, but the strategic position of most of their islands meant that freebooters, whalers, blackbirders and traders were inevitably followed by the official claim-staking of both European and Asian nations. For the high islands of the Mariana group lie in a north-south line and serve as stepping stones out of Asia into the Pacific. South of them the Caroline archipelagoes spread like a net from east to west for some 2000 miles (3500 kilometres). Farther east the low-lying atolls of the Marshall and Kiribati groups, together with the Polynesian Tuvalu, form a con-

tinuous chain of atolls and islands which extend south-eastward into western Polynesia.

The principle protagonists in the area were Spain, Germany, Japan, Britain and America. And the prizes for which they contended were natural resources like the phosphates of Nauru and Banaba; the copra; the shell and the fish and, in the case of Japan, space for surplus population. They built cable stations, naval bases, airfields, and more recently, satellite tracking stations and nuclear test grounds. Present-day independence movements, particularly in Belau and

the Carolines, have stimulated a revival of traditions. For instance, long-distance inter-island voyaging had almost ceased until in 1970, in a symbolic affirmation of island inter-dependence, a five-man canoe from Satawol atoll, using traditional tech-niques of navigation, sailed to Saipan in the northern Marianas where a colony of Caroline Islanders including Satawolese had existed since the early 19th century.

Although the myths of many Micronesian islands have been lost some were recorded by early travel-lers and missionaries, and adminis-

Hipour, a famed navigator of Puluwat in the Caroline Islands, is seated on the navigator's bench on the inner edge of the lee platform. His hand is at the ready on the sheet or heavy coir line used to regulate the angle of sail for the boat and therefore the wind. Inter-island canoe sailing is still important in the region and navigators have the highest status in the community.

Page 70 In Kiribati all community life – whether ceremonial, recreational or in the matter of maintaining law and order – was centred on the great meeting house of *maneaba*. A view of the interior of a *maneaba* on Tabiteuea (Drummond Island) from the fifth volume of *Wilkes Voyages*, 1845. Some of the men are wearing their basketwork body armour. Museum of Mankind, London.

trators like Sir Arthur Grimble in Kiribati. Since the war this knowledge has been supplemented by folklore studies in several places sponsored by CIMA (Co-ordinating Investigation of Micronesian Anthropology), including Ulithi in the western Carolines and Ifaluk, which is a mere speck half a mile square (1.3 square kilometres) in the central Carolines with a population of 260.

In Micronesia, as in Polynesia, rank was of some importance and, especially on the larger and more populous islands, the existence of a leisured class stimulated the development of a rich oral literature. The Chamorro held their poets in special esteem and in their islands there was also a society called the Uritoy which seems to have resembled the Arioi of the Society Islands. Formal schools like those of Polynesia seldom seem to have existed, although the Idan of Truk received strict training in traditional lore and magic and claimed that the sky deity, Anulap, was their founder and teacher.

Myths were sometimes part of the secret lore of a special group such as navigators. On Tibuteuea those who sought to become masters of lore studied composition and actually fished for words from the outer reef. When they felt the inspiration tickle their line they shouted the words and phrases to their supporters on the shore. On Ifaluk it is said that inspiration for a new song comes from the god Tilitr who descends and takes possession of a man or woman.

In many parts of Micronesia cosmogenic myths are rare and even the primal deities, though mentioned, do not seem to be given much attention, but their semi-divine offspring, especially tricksters like Olifat, Motikitik and Nareau are the central characters of many favourite stories, which are often arranged in cycles. The plots of these tales make use of those situations which give rise to tensions within the group, such as problems of land ownership and the difficulty of fulfilling the onerous system of gift exchange by which status is advanced and prestige won. The trickster element is strong in stories about animals and boys who kill ogres.

Though the tales are humorous, the humour has a cutting edge and very often depends on the discomfiture of a victim. Tales in which incest is committed, either knowingly or unknowingly, also occur on many islands.

Creation Stories

The Spaniards wrote that the Chamorro believed in, but did not worship, Puntan, a being 'who existed before sky and earth'. When the time came for him to die he instructed his sister, 'who like himself, was born without either father or mother', to make a place for mankind by using his breasts and back to make the earth and sky, his eyes to make the sun and moon, and his eyebrows to make the rainbow. This use of the parts of a creator's body to make the firmament is a motif which also occurs in the myths of eastern Micronesia. In central Micronesia, however, the people, when they were

concerned about creation at all, assumed that the sky and the world always existed, requiring only to be made habitable.

In the east, in Kiribati and the neighbouring islands of Niue (Tuvalu), Banaba and Nauru, the most widespread belief was that the labour of creation was shared by two beings called Ancient Spider and Young Spider. Variants of their names were Nareau, Naareau, Narleau, Na-arean and Areop-enap. Sometimes the elder Nareau was described as pre-existent, dwelling in

a darkness or void, or floating in endless space, or on an infinite sea. In other accounts creation was said to be the product of the union of abstractions similar to those of the genealogical evolutionary myths of Polynesia. The sequence began with Te Bo Ma, Darkness, and Te Maki, The Cleaving Together. Their descendents were Void, Night, Daylight, Thunder and Lightning, as well as the Younger Nareau, who then carried on with the rest of creation.

In one myth from Kiribati in which

Above East gable of Bai ra Ngesechel a Chercher, Koror, Belau. The Belauan traditional *bai* or men's meeting or council house is, by its architecture, design and decoration, a symbol of Belau culture. The gable pictographs depict mythological events. Symbols found on all *bai* include a cross within a circle, representing Belauan money and the cock whose crowing prevented the completion of the first *bai*. Traditionally a *bai* is built elsewhere and then assembled on site. Neither nails or lashings are used in its construction; it is held together by a complex system of joinery and removeable pegs. This *bai* was built on the west coast of Babeldaob by the cooperative effort of two clubs. Belau National Museum.

Nareau the Elder was a pre-existent being, it was said that he took a tridacna shell and from this made heaven and earth. In another version, translated by Sir Arthur Grimble, heaven was described as a rock which although it was stuck fast to earth sounded hollow. Tapping on it Nareau cried:

Tap, Tap on heaven and its dwelling places!
It is stone. What becomes of it? It answers!
It is rock. What becomes of it? It answers!
Open Sir Stone! Open Sir Rock!
It is open – o – o!

Whereupon Nareau climbed in.

The main primal event described in myths of this type was always the separation of earth and sky – a theme which is shared with Polynesian creation stories. In these islands however, the sky-raiser was not a primal deity but an eel, Riiki, or a worm, Rigi. First Nareau the Elder ordered Sand and Water to mate. Next, two of their offspring produced a multitude of children, including Na Kika the octopus and Riiki, the eel, and the youngest child was again called Nareau. To him was given the task of creation. He looked about him and saw a company of fools and deaf mutes. He shaped their bodies, loosed their limbs and tongues and opened their eyes and ears; but when he called on them to raise the sky they could not do it, so he struck off two of the arms of the octopus, leaving eight, and using them as bait he enticed Riiki to help him. While the eel and the other sea creatures struggled to raise the sky Nareau chanted:

Hark, hark how it groans, the Cleaving Together of old!
Speed between Great Ray, slice it apart.
Hump thy back, Turtle, burst it apart.
Fling out thy arms, Octopus, tear it apart.
West, East, cut them away!
North, South, cut them away!
Lift, Riiki; lift, kingpost of the roof, prop of the sky.
It roars, it rumbles! Not yet, not yet is the Cleaving Together sundered.

While Nareau sang, Riiki pushed up the sky and the earth sank, leaving the fools and deaf mutes swimming in the sea. Then Nareau leapt forward

Right The wheel-sized stone discs known as 'stone money' on Yap were quarried on Belau and had to be transported by canoe across 230 miles (370 kilometres) of open sea. Museum of Mankind, London.

Opposite This bird-shaped container, inlaid with pearl shell, was a gift from 'Abbe Thule', the Ibedul or High Chief of Koror, Belau, to Captain Henry Wilson whose ship, *The Antelope* (an East India packet), was wrecked there in 1783. The local people helped him to build a new ship in return for iron tools and assistance in fighting their enemies. This vessel was said to hold thirty-six English quarts of a sweet drink. Museum of Mankind, London.

and pulled down the sides of the sky so that it was shaped like a bowl. Some say he took four women and placed one at each corner of the heavens to support it. There they became rooted to the spot. The exhausted Riiki died and was flung into the heavens to become the Milky Way. His severed legs fell and populated the ocean with eels. As it was still dark Nareau's work could not be seen, so he took his father's eyes and made them the sun and moon. He crumbled his father's brain and the scattered crumbs became the stars. From his father's flesh he made rocks and stones and from his father's spine grew the Ancestral Tree, Kai-n-tiku-aba, the Tree-of-the-Resting-Place-of-Lands, which stood on Samoa. From the branches of this tree sprang the ancestors of men who were known as the Breed of Matang. Amongst this company of ancestors were Taburimai and Au-ria-ria.

In other myths, in which Nareau has the role of a trickster rather than a creator, Taburimai sometimes appears as a foil. On the island of Nui, Tabakea the turtle is described as the 'father of all things' and although Nareau is his son, Au-ria-ria usurped his creative functions.

Nearby Banaba is said to rest on Tabakea's back, because Au overturned the island and thrust the turtle beneath it. Such variations in the roles of the characters of the stories probably reflect the shifts in power amongst the clans who told them.

It is said that Nareau picked flowers from the ancestral tree and flung them to the north of Samoa. Where they floated Tarawa, Beru and Tabuteuea came into being. This charming allusion to the migration of people from Samoa to Kiribati was supported by the belief that two great trees, which stood on the island of Beru, had grown from pieces of the Ancestral Tree. They were referred to as the male and female ancestors of the main tribe, Karongoa, and were treated with due deference until they were cut down by missionaries in 1892.

These creation myths display elements similar to those found in other parts of Oceania. The formlessness of the fools and deaf mutes of these stories is reminiscent of the shapeless maggots which grew from the vine in the creation stories of western Polynesia. In Melanesia, a spider is the companion of Qat, a trickster. Moreover the great mythologist Roland Dixon noted a perhaps more important similarity between this Kiribati creation story and a myth from the Kayan of central Borneo which described a primal deity as a spider into whose web fell a stone which became land. Upon this land grew a worm which made earth. In this earth a tree took root from whose branches grew the ancestors of men.

North of Kiribati in the Marshall Islands, the being who was responsible for creation was Lowa, perhaps a cognate of the Polynesian sea deity-creator god, Tangaloa. He brought the islands into existence by merely making the magical sound 'Mmmmm'. Some said he dwelt in a primeval sea and others said that he came down from the sky. His offspring, a boy and a girl, were born from a blood blister on his leg. But it is not clear whether they were supernatural beings or the first humans. Throughout the area mankind was often described as having been brought into existence by a direct act of creation. On the island of Truk it was Anulap's busy wife, Ligoububfanu, who made men, plants and animals, and the islands as well.

The Way of the Soul after Death

The Micronesians did not have a myth about a hero like Maui who sought to obtain immortality for man. It was usually assumed that the gods had decreed that man should be mortal. The souls of the dead journey either northward or westward to the leaping place which leads either to an island of the dead, or skyward, or underground – opinions vary from island to island. Some Marshall Islanders say that the dead must swim a channel to reach the island of Nako, where the spirit food is everlasting, but some are weighted down by their sins and sink. An association between original sin and man's mortality is even stronger in a Kiribati story, collected by Grimble.

In the beginning, the story goes, men and women lived apart and were innocent. The men had a tree which bore a single nut that was replenished as soon as it was plucked and a fish trap that was always full of fish. The women also had a tree that Nakaa, the guardian, forbade the men to touch. But a day came when, in Nakaa's absence, the men disobeyed him. When he returned he knew this had happened because he smelt the perfume of the women's flowers and saw the men's grey hairs.

'Fools,' he said, 'Death has come amongst you.' And he took the fish trap and the tree of life and left them.

He went to the entrance of the spirit world and there he sat weaving a net and catching the souls of the dead in its flying strands. The wrong-doers were condemned to struggle in everlasting entanglement, but the good were free to join their ancestors. Another version claimed that if a ghost could refrain from eating the fruit from the inexhaustible tree and the food from the fish trap, and if he could resist drinking the water from the never-empty well, for three days, he could return to the living.

The story of Nakaa and the trees recalls the Tree of Knowledge of the Garden of Eden and the idea of retribution after death seems Christian rather than Oceanic, but other

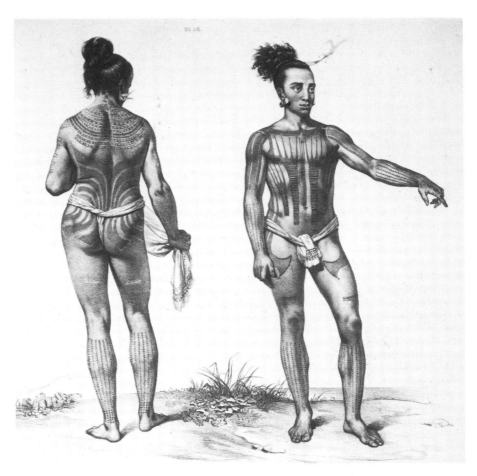

elements such as an inexhaustible food supply are particularly Micronesian and also occur in Melanesian and Polynesian myths.

Land Fishing and other Feats: Motikitik and his Mother Lorop

Heroic feats of sky raising, land-fishing, fire-stealing and regulating the sun's progress – which in Polynesia are most frequently attributed to Maui – are not great Micronesian themes nor are they linked together in narrative cycles about one person. Maui reappears in Micronesia as Motikitik but confines his activities almost completely to fishing up food and land. Some Kiribati myths tell of a son of Nareau called Maturang who fished up land but in eastern Micronesia land-fishing and the supervision of lifting the sky are usually amongst the creative tasks performed by Nareau. Sometimes Nareau even bears the epithet Tekikitea, Tekitekite or Tekikinto, the Micronesian equi-

valent of Maui's *tikitiki*.

Another method of creating land, by strewing sand from a coconut shell, was popularly told in the eastern Caroline Islands. But the motives of the strewer seem to have been relatively mundane. William Lessa has recorded the story of a woman who went off in a huff because she was always being scolded, or slighted by her relatives, or given short rations. As well as casting sand on the water to make an island she sometimes made food in the new land by squeezing milk and shavings over the ground.

On the island of Yap both explanations of land-making were given. It was said that Liomarar strewed sand to make the nearby island of Ulithi. She then had a daughter called Lorop, who had three sons, the youngest of whom was Motikitik. Each day when the sons returned from fishing they found that Lorop had prepared great quantities of food from an unknown source. One day Motikitik stayed home and spied on his mother. He heard her utter a spell and then she

74

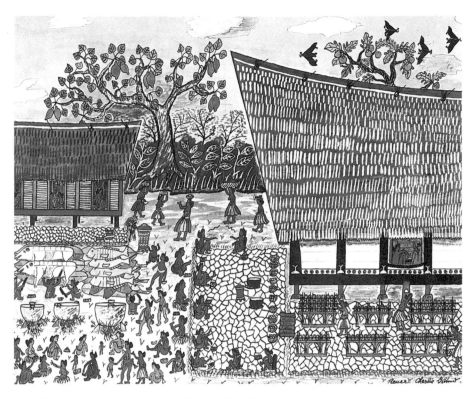

dived into the sea. Transforming himself into a bird, he followed her and saw her gathering food in the underworld. Alas, the discovery of his mother's secret meant her death. She told him to bury her and return with the food as usual, without telling his brothers what had happened. Motikitik obeyed her.

On the following three days while the brothers were fishing Motikitik fished up baskets of food, and on the fourth day he fished up the island of Fais. When his brothers quarrelled with him about the ownership of the new land he suggested that their mother should arbitrate, so they visited her grave. Each brother asked the grave to whom the land belonged but only Motikitik received the answer: 'Mmmmm'. So Motikitik chose to live in the middle of the island and the other brothers occupied opposite ends. The myth therefore explains the origin of the three districts of Fais.

Far from being a trickster like his Polynesian namesake Maui-tikitiki, Motikitik seems a rather solemn fellow who uses his special powers to make himself a man of property. A sequel to this story is the belief that Motikitik later lost his land-fishing hook which eventually fell into the hands of the powerful village of Gatschapar on Yap. Tradition has it that if the hook is lost, Fais will sink to the bottom of the sea. Fear of this happening has kept the people of Fais in subjection to the people of Yap to whom they, and other neighbouring islands, pay tribute.

In Kiribati the sun-snarer was a hero called Bue, who attacked the sun at six stopping places with six missiles, the last of which was a coconut leaf which he used as a snare. Each object he threw at the sun reduced its heat but this was not his main objective, for what Bue wanted from the sun was knowledge. He was given the staff, Kai-ni-hamata, which Grimble and others thought might be a corrupt form of Kai-ni-kamaka or fire-stick. If this is so, sun-snaring and fire-quest themes are united in this one myth. Fire was also brought from heaven in other Micronesian stories, instead of from underground, as in Polynesia. From Nauru comes the story of Young Spider who demanded the fire-stick from the woman, Lightning, and then broke the arm of her husband, Thunder, when he tried to recover it. In the central Carolines it was the trickster, Olifat, who sent a bird down to earth with fire in its beak, to place it in different trees so that men might obtain it by rubbing two sticks together.

The Exploits of Olifat

Although Olifat was known as a bringer of benefits and skills to mankind he was above all a notorious trickster whose pranks at best made fools of men, and at worst caused their injury or death, his sole object being to assert his superiority of birth and to prove the power of his magic. Lessa has carefully analysed the many variations of the theme in *Myths from Ulithi Atoll*.

The variations in his name throughout the Carolines are many, including Yelafath, Iolofath, Orofat, Wolphat. He is the son of a mortal woman and a sky deity who is sometimes called Lugeiläng (Lukelong, Luk or Great Yelafath), and the sky deity Anulap (Analap, Onolap, Enulap) is his grandfather. Sometimes Anulap is his father and then Lugeiläng is his brother.

The Ulithians say that when Lugeiläng went down to earth to court a woman, his heavenly wife tried to follow him and prevent the union, but at each attempt the mortal's mother, Hit, the octopus, performed an erotic

dance which caused the sky-wife to die – presumably of embarrassment at such bold behaviour – and her attendants carried her back to heaven. Like most heroes and tricksters Olifat had a most unusual birth. His mother pulled on a twist of coconut leaf rib which was tied round a lock of her hair – and the child came forth from her head.

All narrators agree that the miraculous child was precocious and fast-growing. In Ifaluk they say he ran as soon as he was born, and wiped the birth blood off on the palm trees which have remained a reddish colour ever since. His father Lugeiläng had warned his mother that the boy should never be allowed to drink from a coconut through a small hole; but one day he did so, and as he tipped his head back to drain the last drop he saw his father in heaven. Immediately he wanted to visit him.

He made the journey on a column of smoke that rose from a fire of coconut shells. His reception in heaven was not a happy one, for on each of the first three levels of the sky-land, *Lang*, the children refused to let him join in their games. On the first level he caused their playthings, the scorpion fish, to grow spines which pricked the boys' fingers; on the second level he made the sharks' teeth grow, for until then they had had none. On the third level he caused the stingrays, which until then had been harmless, to develop stingers. At last he arrived at the fourth level where people were busy helping his father to build a Färmal, or house for the spirits of the dead.

Olifat helped to dig the posthole. His father pretended that he did not know him, and the other men decided to kill the boy because he was a stranger. But Olifat guessed their intentions and made a hollow to one side at the bottom of the hole. When the men rammed the post down the boy retreated into the cavity and squirted first a mouthful of red earth and then some chewed green leaves, so that the men thought it was his blood and gall they saw. Confident that the boy was dead, they filled in the hole.

Meanwhile Olifat, helped by the termites, tunnelled through the post and climbed into the rafters. He asked the ants to fetch him a piece of coconut and a piece of taro. They returned with very small pieces indeed, but Olifat caused them to grow to full size. Then dashing one against the other, he cried: 'Soro!' As this is a word which one uses when one comes before a superior, the men were afraid when they heard the cry. They looked up and saw the boy they believed dead perched in the rafters. Then his father saw him and ordered him to come down. So began the adventures of Olifat, which took him through all levels of *Lang* as well as back to earth.

This attempt to murder Olifat in the posthole inevitably calls to mind the almost universal folk belief that a human sacrifice should be sealed in the foundations of a building to give it strength. However the practice has not been recorded in the Caroline Islands and none of the stories about Olifat suggest that he was chosen to be a sacrifice. But the implication of a sacrifice is there, for the choice of a stranger for such a purpose was a natural one.

Anyway he was a very aggravating fellow. He fouled other men's coconut toddy, swapped bad food for good, spoiled fishing expeditions, and was an incorrigible seducer. Not even the wives of his relatives, including Anulap himself, were safe from him. On Ifaluk they tell how he turned himself into a mosquito and was swallowed by his brother's wife in her drinking water. Olifat was born as her son and in this way gained access to her.

Many a tale about Olifat was spun out by elaborating on the many transformations he used to avoid detection or punishment. In one tale a hapless husband searched for the intruder but each time he found only a bird, a pile of dung, a coconut or some other object. At last, after he was advised to shoot at anything which moved, he shot at a quivering leaf. Whereupon Olifat materialised and ran away laughing. It is little wonder that he was squashed in postholes, burned,

mnemonic – aid to memory

shot at and cast into the sea in a fish trap.

Yet his advice was sought in affairs of love. A favourite story in many islands tells how he helped a handsome man recover a beautiful wife by using some charmed tumeric to lure her back to him at a dance. And on Ifaluk they claim that Olifat introduced the art of tattooing, which has erotic significance for these islanders because they apply it to the genitals. In a story recorded by E. G. Burrows the islanders tell of a woman who fell in love with Olifat because she admired his tattoo designs. The other women saw him too, and woke their husbands that they might see his beauty. Next morning, when he returned to the sky, the men painted the same patterns on themselves with charcoal. The next night Olifat returned without the designs (as he was a god he could easily remove them), and the woman rejected him. Undeterred, he slipped outside and put them on again and returned to her favour. The following day he taught the people how to use the tattooing needle so their patterns would be permanent.

Olifat's most vicious prank was the murder of his brother. After he had been staying with his father for a while he discovered that he had a brother whose existence had been kept from him. This boy lived in the third heaven and each night he went fishing and dutifully brought the catch to his father. One night Olifat trapped his brother, cut off his head, and left it for his father in place of the usual offering of fish. The father was very angry. He restored his elder son's head to his body and chastised Olifat, but that wicked one pretended surprise and complained: 'You said I had no brother – so how could I have killed him?'

There are other stories about Olifat and his brother which are reminiscent of stories about rival brothers, one filial or handsome and the other evil or stupid, which are so popular in Melanesia.

In Kiribati where Olifat was unknown, Nareau assumed his characteristics and had similar adven-

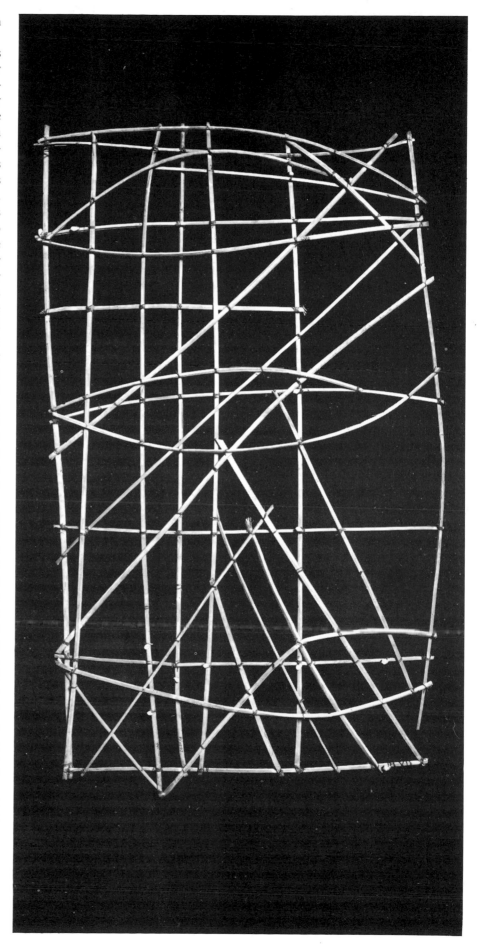

tures. He used his spider form to escape death in the posthole. Special problems arose for him as a foot-loose god, wandering in the land of men without his own trees for toddy, gardens, property or any of the things which gave a man status. The Tabute-ueans told how Nareau was challenged to an exchange of food in the *maneaba* (meeting house). With the help of his insect friends he resorted to scavenging the food crumbs from the women's sleeping mats in their bleaching house and he made up the weight of his gift package with excrement. When his filthy trick was discovered he ran off with everybody in hot pursuit, but not before he and the insects had eaten all the other fellows' food. When he was almost overtaken at the edge of the outer reef he dropped sharp coral and shells and poisonous sea urchins to hinder his pursuers.

In a society in which food scarcity was not uncommon and an insistence on formal codes of behaviour and the complex system of gift exchange caused considerable social pressures, the very offensiveness of these stories provided a release for audience and narrators alike.

Animals as Tricksters and Animals as Helpers

Stories about animals as tricksters usually involve a basic cast of three characters. Favourites are the rat, the land crab and a turtle or octopus. One familiar story tells of a land crab and a rat having a quarrel, because the rat either refuses to share food or toddy, or fouls it before handing it over. The land crab waits until they go sailing before he takes his revenge and then he makes a hole in the canoe and walks off along the ocean floor, leaving the rat to drown. Along comes an octopus who offers to carry the rat to the shore. On the way the rat chews his bearer's hair. After he is safely ashore he jeers at the octopus for being bald. Sometimes the benefactor fares much worse, even being fouled by the animal he carries. In one tale the benefactor is a turtle, and the rat summons all the animals to help him kill and eat the creature who has rescued him.

Tricks like these are said to explain the everlasting enmity which is said to exist between these animals. On many islands an imitation rat is used as bait for the octopus because it is known that they are sworn enemies. This type of animal tale exists throughout Oceania, but is even commoner in Malaysia. In Micronesia the animal trickster is always the rat.

There is another kind of animal tale told in Micronesia in which an animal mother, usually a lizard, contributes food to her human daughter and this increases the family's prestige. Eventually the husband demands to meet his mother-in-law and when he does he takes pity on her and is kind to her. The Melanesians tell a similar story about a generous animal relative, usually a snake, but the conclusion is fundamentally different. The husband, horrified by the discovery, kills the animal relative, his wife and family, and then commits suicide.

The Ogre-killers

The favourite bogeymen of Micronesian islands are cannibal spirits or ogres who are characterised by their brute strength and their stupidity. They tend to come in families of ten; ten brothers, each one hand-span taller than the next, or the first with one head and the second with two heads and so on. They can sometimes be driven away by blowing on a conch trumpet or simply by making lots of noise. Fire destroys them too. Very often they have kindly mothers who help their victims to escape. Common delaying tactics used by an escapee are to ask coconut shells or bananas on a bunch to answer for him, or to drop objects with powerful magic such as hair or spittle. Very often the ogre's death is brought about by a trick.

In one story two children are almost overtaken by an ogre. They hide in a hollow bamboo and persuade the foolish fellow to pull out his gut so that they can draw him into the hollow after them. In this way they kill him. In another, a man who is considered simple-minded by his fellows allows himself to be caught, then delays his death by first suggesting to the ogre that they have a little drink, then a feast so that he will be fatter and better eating. Finally he suggests a game of hide and seek, during which he traps the ogre in a spring made by bending down a coconut tree. The coconut tree snaps upright, leaving the ogre hanging by one leg above a fire that burns him to death.

Sometimes the ogres who dwell in the bush so terrorise a district that it has to be abandoned. This calls for the birth of an ogre-slaying child, who is a special hero in Melanesia but is also well-known in Micronesia. The Ulithians told a tale of a boy who slays ogres to the folklorist William Lessa.

The villagers decided to go away because the ogres were gradually eating everybody. As each canoe party left, a poor woman without relatives tried to join it but was pushed away. Finally she was left alone in the village and hid in a hole under a tree. Although the ogres divined that a human was still there they could not find her. Very soon she gave birth to a child who grew so fast he was soon as large as a boy of thirteen; but he had only one leg. One day this boy disobeyed his mother's instructions and went in search of the ogres. He came upon their mother cooking a meal while they were fishing. He upset the pot and ate the food. The next day one ogre stayed at home to protect the mother but the boy came again and killed the ogre by slicing off his head with his sharp thumb-nail. He set the body on the beach for the returning brothers to see. They were angry when they found their brother was dead and the next day the next brother waited for the boy. Once again the boy severed his head with his thumb-nail. The same thing happened on each of the following days until all the ogres were dead. Then the woman and her son walked on the beach so that the villagers, who now lived on the neighbouring island, could see them and know that it was safe to return. The villagers were so overjoyed when they returned and discovered the ogres were dead that they made the boy their chief.

Pälülop's Family of Seafarers

The Marshall Islands version of the myth about two brothers, Rongerik (small cheeks) and Rongelap (large cheeks), who lend their names to two islands in that group, has been lost but stories about the brothers and the very large family of seafaring deities to which they belong have been recorded from one end of the Caroline Islands to the other. There are bewildering variations in the names of the different family members as well as shifts in relationships and attributes. Very often Pälülop, the great canoe captain, is said to have been the father of the family and his most distinguished son is Aluluei. Sometimes the relationships are reversed, but whether he is father or son, Alulei is always the great teacher and patron of the arts of navigation.

The people of Ifaluk say Aluluei is the father of two brothers who were known to them as Longorik, the younger and Longolap, the elder. They tell how the father gave the two boys lessons in seamanship but Longolap was inattentive because he had just got married. Because of his

Above A young Belauan woman celebrates the birth of her first child.

Opposite A table for offering food to the gods, decorated with inlaid pearl shell, from Belau. Museum of Mankind, London.

failure to learn properly his brother was always having to rescue him. One day the young men cut a breadfruit tree to make a canoe but it magically went together again, as did the tree that the Polynesian hero, Rata, cut. At last Longorik learnt from his father that a little bird that was sitting near the tree was really Solang, the god of carpenters, in disguise. Indeed the bird uttered the high, trilling note that gods make. The boys enlisted his aid and he sent them to ask the women to make pandanus-mat sails. While they were away the god summoned the ants to finish and launch the canoe.

Longorik told his father that he wanted to visit the sands of Aluluei (presumably the island which, in other myths, Aluluei made). His father warned him that he must not let the spirits who live there tie up his boat, and if they offered him a choice of clean or dirty water to bathe in, he must choose the dirty. He advised him to place two pieces of coconut meat on his eyelids at night so that he would appear to be awake. Finally he told him to ask for Aluluei's stone. All these are motifs which occur in other Oceanic tales about voyages to strange lands.

Longorik was about to embark when his brother came to the beach and insisted that he should be the first to make the journey, and he set sail, leaving Longorik behind. When

Longolap arrived at the island he let the apparently friendly spirits help him and did everything contrary to his father's advice, so that during the night he and his men were walled up in the round end of the house. Longorik set out to rescue him. Arriving at the island, he meticulously observed his father's instructions, and after surviving the night unharmed he asked the spirits to fetch Aluluei's stone. While they were away he released his brother's party and together they escaped.

On many other islands these two brothers are barely mentioned, or perhaps the myth has been lost, and other members of the family take centre stage. The series of myths about them are extraordinarily complex. There are often said to be seven sons and sometimes the locale shifts from sky to earth after a family quarrel over the borrowing of adzes. The departing son and his wife take the parents' names as pseudonyms and give their children their brothers' names. One of the less confusing versions comes from Lamotrek in the central Carolines.

In this story Pälülop was said to be the father, and his two sons, Big Rong and Little Rong were great rivals until a third son, Aluluei, was born. He was said to have acquired wisdom while he was yet in his mother's womb. The older brothers, jealous of Aluluei, killed him and threw his weighted body into the sea; but the father brought the boy back in spirit form. As a protection he provided him with numerous eyes which shone like stars. First he told Aluluei to steal the brothers' possessions and then, when the boys complained to him about the unseen thief, he advised them to build a canoe with a hut on it which would be sure to attract the culprit.

Indeed Aluluei liked the canoe his brothers built so much that he sailed away in it with the aid of a crew of forty rats. This greatly puzzled the brothers Rong, who couldn't see the rats and wondered how a single man could manage such a craft. Aluluei took sand with him and a pandanus tree. He scattered the sand to make an island and he planted the tree. He took the hut from the boat and lived in it.

Pälülop had a fourth son, Faravai. One day while out sailing he made an offering of fish skins and coconut shells to his brother Aluluei. This meanness made Aluluei so angry that he failed to protect his brother in a storm and when Faravai was wrecked on his island he offered him the same poor food. Later Aluluei relented and gave him a very small drink which was nonetheless thirst-quenching. On another occasion Faravai cut up a fish he had caught and as he did so the same portions of Aluluei's body disappeared until only his skeleton was left. Thus Aluluei taught him certain food tabus. After a while Faravai wanted to go home but his brother demanded that he should first delouse his hair. Faravai was terrified by the eyes he saw hidden in the hair, but Aluluei explained that they were stars and taught him their names so that he became a great navigator. After other adventures, in which his canoe of sand disintegrated, Faravai arrived home on the back of a turtle.

Pälülop's family were probably the most important mythological characters in Micronesia. The islanders placed amulets and offerings to Aluluei in the small sacred hut which was built over the outrigger of their fast sea-going canoes. Some said he lived on sand-bars. Others said he had two faces, one of which looked forward and saw what men saw, and one which looked back and saw approaching dangers. Solang, the patron of canoe builders, and in some islands the teacher of house-building and the art of making boxes with lids, was also worshipped.

The Porpoise Girl

A popular theme in Micronesia is that of a girl who comes either from the sea or the sky to watch men dance or to steal something. She is prevented from returning home because a man hides either her wings or her tail. The Ulithians tell how two porpoise girls came ashore to watch men dance.

Each night they shed their tails and hid them. On the fourth night a man who had seen strange marks on the beach spied on them and stole one girl's tail so that she could not return to the sea. The man married her and hid the package which contained her tail in the rafters. After a while she had two children and seemed content. Then one day, bugs falling from the rafters directed her attention to the parcel. She opened it, and finding her tail put it on. Before returning to the sea she warned her children that they must never eat porpoise meat.

This simple tale conveys perfectly the islanders delight in the narrative art. Yet it is more than an idle tale for almost always the story is used to explain the origin of certain food tabus or social customs. It is also significant in another way, for some mythologists consider that it belongs to the tale-type defined as 'Swan Maiden'; the basis of which is that a supernatural girl loses her wings and is forced to remain on earth as the wife of her captor. One day she recovers them and makes her escape. Her husband follows her and attempts to win her back. Sometimes he succeeds.

This is a theme of tremendous antiquity; elements of it are to be found in a story from the Indian *Rig Veda*, recorded 3000 years ago. Its widespread distribution in Oceania and even Australia also points to its early arrival in the area, and consideration of those story-elements which persist and those which are lacking in the different places is an interesting exercise in comparative mythology. The folklorist William Lessa has pointed out that only one Micronesian story includes the episode of the husband's search for his wife. Malaysian examples of this theme on the other hand tend to be elaborate; there is also a Melanesian version which contains a story element which links it with an episode in the Polynesian cycle of myths about Tawhaki and Rata, in which the searcher visits the sky world and meets his old blind grandmother counting yams.

Melanesia

Myth and Change

In many parts of Melanesia, particularly Vanuatu, the encroachments of the Europeans took place with the same mixture of brutality and indifference that marked the process elsewhere in the Pacific. In other places, especially in New Guinea, the encounter was more gradual and even today there are isolated communities where contact remains minimal. In these communities the way of life of the people has been hardly touched by the ways of the European, and their myths, especially in their ritual re-enactment, continue to reinforce the intricate bond between themselves and nature upon which their survival depends. Yet such mythological systems are not static; they reflect the limited social change which occurs continually in all societies no matter how isolated. In the many other Melanesian societies that are in transition and have been affected by contact with a culture as vastly different as the European, myth has a dynamic role as an accessory to social change. And attempts to explain the white man's coming and his superior material culture are often based on old mythological themes.

The people of Tangu who live in a scattering of hamlets not far inland from the north coast of New Guinea have a myth about a certain woman who had no husband to protect her. One day she left her daughter alone and a stranger came and killed the child and buried the body. The woman learnt the whereabouts of the grave in a dream. She recovered the body, and carrying it in her string bag, wandered from village to village until she found a place to bury it and a man, the younger of two brothers, who would marry her. She had two sons by her new husband.

By and by she visited the daughter's grave. Parting some coconut fronds she found salt water flowing from the grave, and fish swimming. The woman took some water and a small fish as food for her family. The results were miraculous. Overnight her son grew to manhood. Her husband's elder brother was envious and wanted the same for his son, so she directed him to the grave. Instead of taking a small fish the foolish man seized a large eel-like one. Immediately the ground quaked and water thundered forth from underground, forming the sea and separating brother from brother. After a while the two brothers re-established contact by floating messages to each other written on leaves. It soon became apparent that the younger brother was able to invent and make wonderful things like boats with engines, umbrellas, rifles and canned food while the elder brother could only make copies. The narrator's conclusion was that this was why some people were black and ate yams.

For the people of Tangu this was no idle tale, nor was it a recollection of past beliefs for the benefit of a stranger. It was one of the several versions of a myth offered the visiting ethnologist Dr. K. Burridge in 1952, in conversations about the rites of the cargo cult they had performed the previous year with the object of obtaining the white man's goods or 'cargo' for themselves. It is not really possible to say why the Tangu chose this particular theme of the release of the sea but perhaps it is worth seeing how it is handled elsewhere in

Orator's 'stool', Korovo ceremonial house, Sepik River, Papua New Guinea. The men's ceremonial house was frequently the scene for great debate over genealogical matters and details of mythology. The speaker stood in front of the orator's 'stool', and as he made a point he struck it with a bunch of leaves.

Melanesia. For the way in which myths change under stress of contact demonstrates well the how and why of myth-making: the way in which elements are re-aligned, re-interpreted and invented.

This theme of the release of the sea is widely known all over Melanesia and is obviously of considerable antiquity. On the island of Dobu in Massim, New Guinea, it was believed that when the sea was released all the beautiful women were swept in a flood to the neighbouring Trobriand Islands while the ugly women were scattered inland in Dobu. Thousands of miles away the inhabitants of Tanna in southern Vanuatu claimed that a woman had a son by a snake who held her captive. At last she poisoned him. A sweet stream of water flowed from his grave and the first coconut tree grew from his eyes. She bathed her son in the water, oiled him and fed him on nuts to make him sleek and fat. One day she discovered that he had disobeyed her and let the other children into the secret. She became very angry and knocked down the containing wall, releasing the sea. The people were scattered to the other islands and the coconuts were carried away to propagate elsewhere. Another Vanuatuan story about the release of the sea accounted for the division of the inhabitants into 'bush' folk and 'salt water' folk.

In these examples and in many others like them the consequences that flow from certain kinds of anti-social behaviour or disobedience seem to be much more important than the explanation of how the sea originated. So it is not surprising that in many other places besides Tangu this type of myth has been adapted and re-interpreted to account for the differences between white and black men. In the Tangu myth the elder brother's misuse of a cultural gift condemns him to a position of inferiority and a state of ignorance. In a variant from the southern Massim district of New Guinea downright deception of one party by another is given as the cause. The story goes that members of two clans together cut down a tree and the sea flowed out. While one group rested and danced the other stole all the 'goods' and floated away with them in the tree trunk. The Europeans were identified as the returning members of this clan.

Clearly these elements of the myth are recent adaptations. They reflect an historical event: the arrival of the white man with his astounding array of material possessions. Yet, expressed as a myth, this event has been placed outside time. What the myth-makers have been attempting to do is to accommodate the new experience within the framework of their traditional beliefs. Not only must the relationship between the white and the black man be established – for they cannot conceive of his being unrelated – his incomprehensible conduct in withholding goods from a brother must also be justified. Knowledge of the white man's technology is lacking, so the myth provides the sanction for attempting to control the situation magically, and the associated ritual of the cargo cult is aimed at recovering 'lost possessions' or redistributing goods more equitably.

Diversity in the Melanesians' View of the World

Before the coming of the European the Melanesian's knowledge of the world seldom extended beyond his immediate neighbours with whom he traded and fought. Amongst the semi-nomadic Arapesh who lived on the mountains to the north of the Sepik River in New Guinea the world was vaguely thought of as an island, if the problem was considered at all. The coastal Busama of the Huon Gulf saw

their district as the centre of a world shaped like an upside-down plate, and believed that anybody who travelled beyond the neighbouring territories had to climb the vault of heaven which was 'solid like thatch'.

The Trobrianders, who were fine sailors and took part in extensive overseas trading expeditions, had a broader world view that encompassed the few hundred square miles of ocean which they called Pilolu. Beyond this to the south and west were the lands of people with wings and people with tails; to the north they knew vaguely of a country of ordinary men – probably New Britain – and another extremely dangerous land, the island of women.

Each small community had its own unique way of looking at the world. Each had its own coterie of mythological beings whose names were seldom known beyond its borders. But the events in which these beings were involved tended to be associated with a number of shared archetypal themes. The way in which stock incidents, elements and themes of myths became linked in a kaleidoscopic variety of combinations derives from the pattern of settlement.

This was one of independent development of innumerable small communities in relative isolation – a process which was constantly modified by external pressures such as minor migrations, warfare, trade and inter-tribal social gatherings, thus ensuring the continuous diffusion of all sorts of cultural elements, including myths.

This cultural diversity is underlined by the variety of languages spoken.

There are a number of Austronesian languages and some 800 Papuan languages whose grouping together stems mainly from their non-Austronesian characteristics. People of Papuan stock predominate in the New Guinea highlands and a scattering of Papuan elements, including languages, are found in some nearby islands as well as in New Britain and

Above The small *mbure*, or god-house, made from sennit sometimes housed sacred objects. It was shaped like the larger temples, but some had woven ears and a mouth which enabled the priest to address the god and hear his reply. Sometimes the god's 'voice' would issue from the *mbure*. In Fiji the priest was regarded as the mouthpiece of the god. Horniman Museum, London.

Opposite, top Shallow pedestal dish in the form of a flying duck from the island of Kadavu, Fiji. Kept in the sacred enclosure, it was used to hold scented annointing oil. Suva Museum, Fiji.

Opposite, bottom On Florida in the Solomons a *tindalo*, the spirit or ghost of a dead man who in his lifetime possessed great *mana* or power, was believed to retain it after death. Sometimes a rough image was set up on a sacred spot associated with him. The *tindalo* did not enter the image, but it served as a focus for approaches of a propitiatory and supplicatory nature. Pitt Rivers Museum, Oxford.

New Ireland and the northern Solomons. The language spoken, however, does not necessarily indicate the stock from which a particular group is derived. Some Papuans are Austronesian speakers and vice versa. A Papuo-Austronesian population predominates towards the eastern extremity of New Guinea and the neighbouring small archipelagoes.

The farther one moves south the more elements predominate which are called Melanesian, though distinctions can be made between coastal and bush people. Polynesian influences are apparent in Fiji and Vanuatu and in the eastern Solomon Islands. Micronesian influence has been felt along the north-eastern edge of the area and the continued movement into the area from the west in the pre-European contact era is indicated by the presence in western New Guinea of Bronze and Iron Age cultural elements.

Most Melanesians are skilled gardeners, pig-raisers and fishermen, but there are exceptions. In the interior of New Guinea there are semi-nomadic tribes who depend on hunting and food-gathering. In the south-western coastal area sago provides the staple crop. In many coastal districts fishing is the basis of the economy.

There are examples of hereditary chieftainship in Melanesia, particularly in New Caledonia and Vanuatu, but social control by a consensus of adult male opinion is much more usual. The Melanesians do not possess the sort of social stratification typical of Polynesia, where a nobility had a vested interest in establishing their descent from the gods. The typical Melanesian, if such a person exists, is not concerned with a hierarchy of deities nor does his mythology unfold a sequence of creation. So earthbound is he that he neglects almost completely the more 'elevated' themes which inspire the myths of Polynesia and Micronesia. He is not so much concerned with the origin of all men as with the origin of his own social unit, his clan, his moiety or his totem. For this knowledge establishes his identity and defines his mode of behaviour; it determines whom he calls brother, and whom he may marry and the young people for whom he is responsible. Throughout the region belief in the efficacy of supernatural beings, both spirits of non-human origin and ancestral spirits, provides the foundation for religious beliefs and practices in all their various local forms.

Myths of Origin and Identity: The Predecessors of Men

Melanesian cosmological beliefs tend to be vague and unformulated but most Melanesians do conceive of a time 'in the beginning' when mythical beings dwelt on earth. The Dobuans say these *Kasa Sona* are ageless and that they were born with the sun, the moon and the earth, whereas 'We are but newly come!' The Keraki Papuans use the word *Gainjin* to indicate that the first beings were 'larger than life'. In some places these primal beings came from the sky, in other places they emerged from underground or merely came from somewhere else. The world was apparently already in existence but they did play a part in shaping it. Sometimes this included raising the sky. Almost always it included making or releasing the sea. Land-making was widely attributed to these beings but their efforts were usually restricted to a particular piece of land rather than *all* land and almost everywhere spirit beings and culture heroes had strong associations with particular localities, conspicuous landmarks and geographical features which they were said to have made.

The Iatmül of the Sepik River area say that the dry land was created when a spirit put his foot upon mud. In Buka, two beings, one male and one female, paddled by and when he steered he made the shorelines straight and when she steered she made it indented. Nuga the crocodile of Kiwai cut the rivers of the estuary with the lashing of his great tail when he discovered that his wife had been seduced. Fijian heroes dropped stolen mountains to make islands and widened channels by straddling them and pushing the lands apart.

Beliefs about man's origin were just as various. Some myths say he came into the world fully grown either from the sky or from underground or was released from a tree. Other myths say he was created from clay or sand or was carved from wood or that he developed spontaneously from stones, maggots, sand drawings, blood clots, eggs or plants.

Very often man shared pride of first creation with another object, plant or animal. According to G. Landtman the Masingle division of the Kiwai Papuans said that a wallaby was killed by 'the first person in the world' and that men grew from the maggots in the corpse while the first gamoda, a plant like kava, grew from the navel. The 'old woman' taught men how to use the gamoda and forbade those who drank it to eat the wallaby because it was their 'father'.

These mythical beings who acted as creators were not the sole creators, for each clan or sub-clan within the group had its own view. For example other Kiwaians believed that their 'father' was the crocodile and a modern account of this story has been written by Mea Idei from Boze near the Binaturi river. He tells how a being called Ipila carved a human figure out of wood and brought it to life by painting the face with sago milk. First the eyes opened, then the nostrils quivered and the 'man' made a noise like a crocodile. But Nugu, for that was his name, was not satisfied until Ipila made three more men as companions for him. These men refused to learn the things Ipila wanted to teach them and turned their backs on him. After a while two of them became tired of only eating sago and started to kill animals for food. Almost at once they turned into half-crocodiles. Neither the animals nor Nugu and the other man wanted any more to do with them so they tried to make some of their own kind. But they found they could only make men because Ipila secretly altered their work. From these new men are descended the people who claim the crocodile as their father. Ipila was so angry with his first creation, Nugu, that he condemned him to hold the earth on his shoulders forever. The narrator concludes that these events explain why his people only know what they know – not why they are alive, nor what is happening beyond their part of the world. (*See* p. 89.)

Descent from the Sky

The idea that there was a sky world which was a replica of this one was fairly widespread in Papua-New Guinea. The Ayom pygmies of the interior told H. Auffenanger that Tumbrenjak climbed down to earth to go hunting and fishing. When he tried to return he found the rope cut. He cried and his wife looked down and cried. Then he set to and built a house. His wife threw down fire and all the fruits and vegetables, including four cucumbers. As soon as the man went off into the bush these turned into four women. When he returned he found all his work done and heard the women's laughter. The offspring of this man and his four wives are the ancestors of the different tribes.

F. E. Williams has recorded the beliefs of the Keraki Papuans of the south-west coast, some of whom say there is a sky world from which the Gainjin came. All agree that they went there when their time on earth was finished; all, that is, except two Gainjin animals, Bugal the snake and Warger the crocodile, who still haunt the bush. An excess of rain is regarded by the villagers as a sign that the sky beings are displeased. They fear that the great rattan cane which supports this aerial world will one day break, so during heavy storms they stand ready to defend themselves in case any of the sky beings should come tumbling down. These beings are appealed to by hunters, fighters and rainmakers.

Release from a Tree

There are two Keraki mythologies, each associated with its own sacred site, and in one of the Kuramangu stories a sky being, Kambel, was curious about the unintelligible sounds which issued from a palm tree and he cut it down, releasing the people. In the evening a shiny white object rose from the palm and slipped from his grasp into the sky. It was his son, the moon. (Both father and son are associated with the moon.)

In another story Kambel despatched one small lizard after another to fetch fire until at last the smallest one succeeded in bringing it back. Kambel then used the fire to roast the pith of the palm and tossed it into the sky to make clouds. These pushed the sky up, though quite how they achieved this isn't clear. In some accounts the animals were also said to come from the great palm and Chel, the python, came from a curled frond-tip. Some say that the rainbow is the great Gainjin Chel himself and others say it is his sloughed skin. The reasons for Kambel and his family's final departure concern a story of incest between mother and son. The father killed the boy and the boy's dog reproached him. Kambel fixed the animal's tongue with a cassowary feather so that it couldn't tell the mother what had happened to her son. From that day onward dogs lost the power of speech. Now they can only howl.

The mountain Kukukuku link two motifs concerning man's origin. They say two brothers killed an opossum and placed its bones in a stream. Gradually these grew into a man. Then one day the brothers found that the man had turned into a tree in which a bird sang. The brothers cut the tree down and the different clans came out singing. The women who were in the valley below climbed up to investigate the noise and were claimed as wives. The brothers named each couple and assigned them their own place to live.

Emergence from Underground
The northern Massim is a relatively homogeneous culture area and there it is believed that the life which existed below ground was exactly like the one above, so that the people who emerged brought with them the rules governing conduct as well as the knowledge of special skills and magic

Right Ceremonial adze with jadeite blade from New Caledonia. Horniman Museum, London.

Opposite A wooden drum, about three and a half feet (a metre) high, from the lower Fly River, Papuan Gulf, New Guinea. Field Museum of Natural History, Chicago, Illinois.

lore. Amongst the Trobrianders, for example, each small sub-clan had an ancestress who emerged with her brother from a particular spot sited in a grove, grotto, lump of coral or rock. With each of these holes of emergence were associated certain territories including garden land and seashore so that each particular myth determined land usage and inheritance. One particular site on the peninsula of Kirawina was especially renowned because from it came the first creatures to emerge on earth. They were the iguana, the dog, the pig and the snake – the animal ancestors of the four principle clans.

Within the area, however, other beliefs both conflicted and merged with these beliefs. Various creative activities were sometimes attributed to Tudava, the roaming culture hero who taught the Trobrianders the techniques and magic of gardening. He distributed the knowledge according to the reception he received in each place, and this is why some lands only grow coconuts while others are rich in yams and other root crops. Some myths claim that Tudava was the first person to emerge in Kirawina, and that as the others came out he gave to each his totem. At that time Kirawina was the only land in existence so Tudava created the neighbouring islands by casting stones into the sea. Other versions of Tudava's life say that he was the child of an abandoned woman who was magically impregnated by a drop of water from a stalactite. The child grew up rapidly and destroyed the ogre who had driven the other people away.

Throughout Melanesia beliefs about origins, not only of men but also of animals, plants, and social customs are frequently linked with certain archetypal themes, one of which is the myth of the ogre-killing child born to an abandoned woman. Other related themes concern abandoned women who mate with animals or birds, or abandoned children who are suckled by animals or birds. Very often one of two hostile brothers or one of a band of brothers is regarded as a creator. Then there are the myths about a snake relative who is killed and from whose body come various forms.

The different ways in which each of these fundamental themes is handled in different places without effecting its basic pattern not only provides a great deal of information about local customs but also illuminates the theme itself.

Snakes as Relatives and Gods

The snake appears in Melanesian mythology as a symbol not only of fertility but also of aggression. He is regarded with an ambivalence that recognises that all creative power is potentially destructive. An aspect of this attitude is demonstrated by the way in which snake beings are said to exercise control over rain. On the one hand they are responsible for the life-giving rain without which the gardens would fail and on the other hand, when provoked, they unleash a deluge and plenty becomes terrifying excess.

From New Guinea to Fiji there are stories about snake relatives who reward kindness or avenge ill-treatment. Sometimes men, animals and plants are produced from their slaughtered bodies. The motif of the growth of the life-giving coconut from the buried head of a snake or eel is as common in Melanesia as in the rest of Oceania, but in this region it is not associated with any particular person like Tuna of Polynesia. Many other snake-beings are wanderers who bestow gifts of new plants, techniques of cultivation and garden magic, and in the south-east Solomons and Fiji snake-beings are given the status of creative deities.

The Arapesh of New Guinea told Margaret Mead of their belief that the spirits or *marsalai* who inhabit the supernaturally charged spots such as rocks, pools and declivities that exist in every clan territory, are sometimes visible as variegated, striped or two-headed snakes or lizards. These snake-beings share certain characteristics with the rainbow snakes of the Australian Aborigines. The *marsalai* are thought vaguely to have been

Left The making of Nugu. In the story of the crocodile men Ipila carved him from a piece of wood and brought him to life by painting his face with sago-milk. A painting by Mea Idei from Boze near the Binaturi River. (*See* p. 86.)

responsible for the customs men practise, and for the shaping of the landscape. More specifically, they are regarded as guardians of the hunting grounds they inhabit and they react malevolently to all trespassers. They are particularly dangerous to childbearing women and can cause miscarriages, stillbirths, illness and death. On the other hand the most effective magic against them derives from menstruating women, when a woman's femaleness is strongest. They cause winds, landslides, earthquakes and flood and there is an Arapesh story about a woman who was the sole survivor of a flood because she had refused to eat any of the eel killed by the other villagers. As a result she acquired the ability to produce yams from her body, much to the advantage of the people she went to live amongst.

Several districts of New Ireland have stories about snakes as food producers and makers of totems and clans. One of these, recorded by H. Powdermaker, comes from the district of Medina and is about Marruni, the earthquake, who had a human body that ended in a snake's tail which he kept hidden from his wives. One day they returned from the garden early without giving the agreed warning signal and discovered him sunning himself. He sent them away and cut his tail into segments. He gave a clan name to some pieces and from each of these came the people of that clan. From others came birds, snakes, fish and pigs. Marruni is said to have come from the tiny offshore island of Tabar, which seems to have been the home of the germinal culture of the area, and to have brought the malanggan or memorial rites for the dead with him from there.

The Mon-alu live on two small islands south of Bougainville and have a culture that is basically Papuan though their language is Austronesian. They have a wandering culture bearer Bunosi, a snake-child of a normal woman, whose great tail filled an enormous house. He was looked after tenderly by his sister Kafisi and when their parents drove him away she went with him. Bunosi made fire for her and coughed up plants and pigs.

Even farther south two snake beings have names resembling Kafisi. They are Kauhausibware of San Cristobal and Koevasi of Florida. The latter is described as a creator from whom all the people of the island are descended. She made many things,

Opposite War trumpet, Sepik, New Guinea. University Museum of Archaeology and Anthropology, Cambridge.

89

including the local dialects, for she was suffering from ague and wherever she went the people copied her confused speech. These two beings belong to a class of spirit called *figona* (*higona*, *vigona*, *hi'ona*) which, in the islands of the south-east Solomons, are associated with those special spots where a man feels awe.

Everywhere in San Cristobal there were stories about serpent *figonas* who were thought to be creators. Hatuibwari of the Arosi district was a winged serpent with a human head, four eyes and four breasts and he suckled all he created. The greatest of all these *figona* was Agunua who was thought to embrace all the others who were merely his representatives or incarnations. He made all kinds of vegetables and fruits but his brother burnt some of these in the oven, making them forever inedible. He made a male child who was helpless at caring for himself so he created a woman to make fire, cook and weed gardens. The first drinking coconut from the tree was sacred to him.

Walutahanga (Eight Fathoms) was a female snake born to an ordinary woman and her story was told on Ulawa, San Cristobal, Guadalcanal, and Florida. It is told in the version given to F. E. Fox. Her mother hid her strange child from her husband, but after she had another child she left the snake-girl to mind the baby while she and her husband went to the garden. The father began to suspect something and one day when he crept back from the garden to spy he heard the snake-girl singing a lullaby:

Ro ruru ro, ia ruro, don't cry,
I have no feet to stand with you,
I have no arms to embrace you,
Ro ruru ro, ia ruro, don't cry.

Horrified by what he saw he chopped her into eight pieces. After eight days rain she was joined together again and began her journeying. She became malevolent and started to pursue and eat people. Again she was cut into eight pieces, and cooked and eaten by everybody except one woman and her child. Her bones were thrown into the sea but they re-united and after another eight showers they were clothed with flesh again. Then Walutahanga summoned up eight huge waves and swept over the village, destroying it. The woman and child were the only survivors and for thcm the snake made yams, taro and coconuts and caused a clear stream to flow; then she went away. Although men were afraid of her 'long evil body and her long crooked tooth' she eventually found a place where she remained as a guardian spirit.

The Fijian deity Ndengei also had a serpent form, though some said his body was stone. He lay coiled in a cavern on Kauvandra mountain and when he turned over the earth quaked. He sent his son Rokomoutu to make the land. Rokomoutu scraped it up from the ocean floor; where his flowing robe trailed across it there were sandy beaches, where he looped it up the coast was rocky. Ndengei hatched two eggs into a boy and a girl and gave them yams and bananas and also taught them the use of fire.

The flood motif was also associated with Ndengei. The story goes that when Ndengei slept it was night and when his black dove woke him daylight came. His nephews who were boatbuilders were tired of working all day long so they shot the dove and prepared to fight Ndengei. He overwhelmed the two brothers with a terrible deluge of rain. As a consequence their clan, the boat-builders, were scattered amongst every tribe. Ceasing to be masters they became the servants of chiefs.

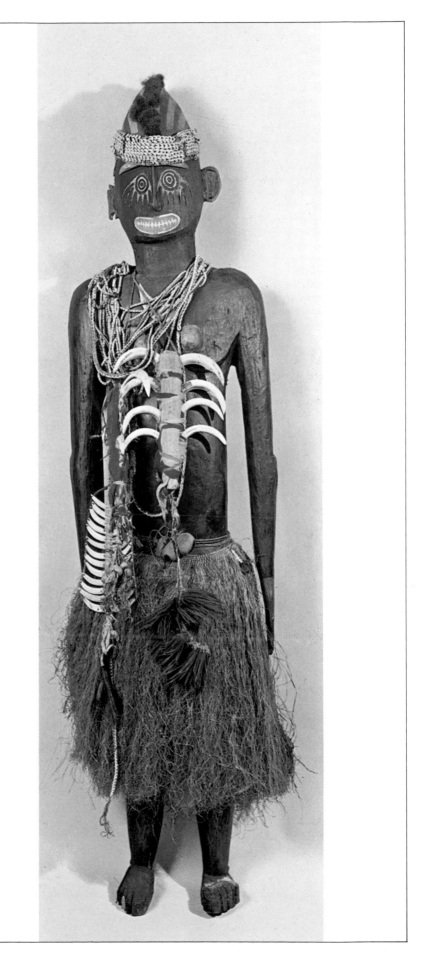

Above The most sacred object possessed by the Namau people of the Purari delta in the Gulf of Papua are the open-mouthed wickerwork monsters called *kaiaimunu*, representing powerful spirits, each with an individual name. This one was photographed by Frank Hurley in 1921, in the partitioned-off section of the kau *ravi* or ceremonial house at Kaimari. These figures were often more than ten feet (three metres) long and seven feet (two metres) high. Part of the initiation of a young boy involved placing him on the *kaiaimunu*, causing it to cave in. After a candidate had helped to make a new figure he was seated in the *kaiaimunu's* jaws and carried about the *ravi*. Some tribes stored bullroarers inside the framework; the sound of these when swung represented the voice of the monster. Other tribes jammed the head or body of a victim of a head-hunting raid into its jaws and then shook it to make it jump with joy and spit it out again. The Vaimuru, a Namau tribe, say that the *kaiaimunu* were given to the Namau by Iko, the culture hero known by many other names – Hido, Sido – throughout the regions of the Papuan Gulf and the Torres Straits.

Opposite An ornament for a sacred bamboo flute, Middle Sepik, New Guinea. Musée de l'Homme, Paris.

The Ogre-killing Child

The theme of the ogre-killing child is common in the western and northern regions and the Massim district of New Guinea, the Bismarck Archipelago, the Solomon Islands and the Vanuatuan islands of Tanna and Malaita. It is apparently absent in Fiji and New Caledonia. Wherever it is told the various motifs associated with the story are remarkably persistent.

The monstrous creature who devours people has many different shapes. He may be an ogre or a giant in human or spirit form, or an animal like the crocodile, snake, osprey, fish hawk or boar. Almost always the ogre-killers are twins, though sometimes there is only one child and occasionally the hero himself is a bird like the cockatoo. Sometimes the ogre-killers and their mother, or very occasionally another relative instead of the mother, are either the sole survivors of the ogre's predatory habits or they are left behind by the fleeing villagers. But most often they are said to have been miraculously conceived by a woman after she has been abandoned. Two lizards may jump down her throat. Possibly her children burst forth from a bud on her forehead or develop from blood from a cut finger. She may mate with various objects or birds. The children grow rapidly and are brave and quick-witted.

The methods they use to kill the ogre are various. The Kamorro of southern Irian who knew about metal tools said that the Varamus, a monstrous bird, was killed when it was lured into a series of houses containing axes, chopping knives, lances, big axes and daggers that magically chopped him to pieces. Occasionally the ogre-killer is identified with a hero who performs other feats. Tudava has been mentioned already and on the Gazelle peninsula, New Britain, the two brothers To Kabinana and To Karvuvu included amongst their exploits the killing of a monstrous pig.

The most significant part of the story is probably the interpretation the narrators themselves place on the theme. The usual implication is that the present-day inhabitants are either the descendants of those who flee from the ogre and later return, or of the ogre-killing children themselves. This idea is explicitly stated in the story of Tsenabonpil from Lesu, New Ireland, as told to H. Powdermaker. The great devouring pig caused the villagers to flee to the offshore island of Tabar, leaving Tsenabonpil behind because she had a swollen leg, so heavy it would have sunk the canoe. She mated with a bird and produced twin boys who killed the pig. The woman sent the pig's hair attached to a coconut leaf to Tabar as a sign. The fugitives returned and Tsenabonpil allocated them to different clans and assigned them their totems so that they would know how to behave towards one another. She also taught them magic and other skills.

All the people of the island of Tanna in southern Vanuatu were devoured by an ogre except one woman who hid under a tree and sustained herself on a root. She swallowed a stone and produced twin boys. They succeeded in killing the ogre Semsem by making him run the gauntlet of a series of weapons spread out across the island. They asked some birds to fly into his wounds and out of his mouth to test if he was really dead. When the birds reappeared their plumage was red, so the twins hacked the body up and the people eaten by the ogre came to life again from the pieces.

The prevalence of this myth about devouring monsters and the return or resurrection of a people – who are then taught the rules of social conduct – is paralleled by the equally widespread practice of initiation rites in which the neophytes are ritually devoured and resurrected or passed through the monster; afterwards they are kept in seclusion while they are instructed in the tribal lore. The symbolic relationship between these two cultural elements is strong, though the actual association between myth and ceremony is usually oblique rather than direct. But a myth from Irian provides a direct association between the ogre-killing theme and the voice of the initiatory monster. It tells how after the twins killed the ogre and buried him, bamboos grew from his grave. Some women heard the wind playing in the stems and they made flutes out of them. When their husbands heard the wonderful sound they killed the women and took the flutes for their secret society. Other instruments used to produce the 'voice' of the monsters are gongs, bullroarers, pipes and distorting devices like bamboos with their ends resting in bowls of water.

In Seniang district of southern Malekula the fearful ogress Nevinbimbaau appears in the myths and also as the presiding spirit of the Nevinbür ceremonies which took place whenever candidates sought admission to the cult society. In the myths she is associated with the great hero-deity Ambat, the eldest of five brothers, who introduced pottery and many social customs such as the making of the commemorative figures for the dead called *rambaramb*. One one occasion Nevinbimbaau was said to have trapped the five Ambat in a deep pit but he led them all to safety along a banyan root. Some say he enslaved the ogress and forced her to carry soil to make an island on the back of a giant clam shell.

Nevinbimbaau was never visible during the Nevinbür ceremonies but

her voice was heard as the booming of the bullroarers which were swung continuously within the sacred enclosure. In *Vanishing Malekula* A. Deacon describes how the Nevinbür ceremonies were staged as a drama before an attentive audience of the uninitiated who sat in front of screens which had been set up between them and the cult house. Nevinbimbaau's grandchildren were the principal cast. Their heads had been modelled on sticks so that they could be manipulated like puppets to show above the screens. In the first act four of these figures were destroyed by an old man who ran forwards and struck at them over the screen with a pig-killing hammer. The second stage lasted several months while the candidates made a great many new figures which were described as 'the thousand maggots new' which arose from the four ghost Nevinbür. Each candidate paid in pigs for the privilege of owning a certain number of these. At the next public performance the candidates danced with these figures over a covered pit in which had been placed a number of old Nevinbür.

Then two special figures with movable forelimbs were fed taro pudding over the screen. In the last act life-sized effigies of Nevinbimbaau's son-in-law Mansip and his two wives were propped in front of the screens and their 'voices' piped through bamboos buried in the ground. Then the old man speared them and their plant-juice 'blood' flowed out most realistically. Finally the effigies cried and groaned as they were burned.

The Hostile Brothers

The central characters in a number of Melanesian myths are two brothers, who although they have different names from place to place tend to be associated with the same mythological themes. They often share the laurels in ogre-killing stories but sometimes victory is achieved because of one brother's superior strength and astuteness. In other stories it is this very difference between the brothers' abilities which determines the outcome of events.

In a tale from Mekeo in New Guinea one brother only has fruit to eat while the other eats meat. The former spies on the latter, and sees him enter a hill which opens at his command and then closes behind him. A little later he emerges with a wallaby and two scrub hens. When the foolish brother tries to do the same thing he is too slow and all the animals escape. The two brothers begin to fight but their wives separate them and send them off to fight an ogre instead.

In some cases one brother's foolishness seems to be merely a foil for the other brother's sagacity. In many others the wise brother's constructive activities are thwarted or diminished by his brother's foolishness, so that the origin of the good things of this world are attributed to the former and the origin of evil to the latter.

In the Bismarck Archipelago the various themes such as land-fishing and the release of the sea, that tend to be told as independent stories in other parts of Melanesia, coalesce around a particular pair of brothers. To Kabinana and To Karvuvu. Like

other wonder-workers they had an unusual birth. They are either described as the children of an abandoned woman, who in her loneliness makes a cut in each of her arms; her children are born from these. Or they are said to have been made by a being who sprinkled two sand drawings of men with blood, then covered them with leaves, and waited for them to grow into real men. These young men created women for themselves out of coconuts, but To Karvuvu threw down his nuts so that the underside – the side without the 'eyes' – hit the ground first, and ugly women with depressed noses emerged. Many harmful consequences are attributed to To Karvuvu's dim wittedness. He made a shark to help him catch other fish more easily and ever since then sharks have eaten both fish and men. When his mother shed her old and wrinkled skin he cried because he did not recognise her youthful appearance, so she looked for her old skin and put it on again. Now men grow old and die. Inability to shed one's skin is the commonest Melanesian explanation of why men die.

Escape from the Posthole

In several places along the north coast of New Guinea and inland amongst the Arapesh there are myths in which the jealousy and rivalry between the two brothers reaches such a pitch that one tries to kill the other by crushing him in a posthole. The choice of this method obviously owes something to the similar story about the Micronesian trickster Olifat.

The Bilibili of Astrolabe Bay include in their stories the episode about two brothers, Manumbu and Kilibob. While Manumbu is away fishing his wife asks his elder brother Kilibob to tattoo her genitals. When her husband returns he sees the design and pours boiling liquid over her. She turns into a turtle and scuttles into the sea. Manumbu then asks his elder brother to help him build a men's club house and to carve a corner post. Kilibob agrees and carves a likeness of his younger brother's wife. Having unwittingly revealed himself as the seducer, Kilibob tries to kill Manumbu by lowering the cornerpost on to him while he is in the hole. But the younger brother makes his

The people of northern New Ireland have a complex of ceremonies known as Malanggan, which are primarily memorial rites for the dead, but also serve as part of the initiation into manhood. A number of carvings of ritual objects, also called Malanggan, are made for a festival. The designs are the property of individuals who instruct the carvers. They make use of mythical and totemic themes as well as actual happenings, and the preparation may take years. The finished figures are gathered together in a special bamboo enclosure and the associated ceremonies, for which special masks are also made, extend over several months. An important prerequisite for a successful festival is a well-stocked garden and an ample supply of pigs. *Above* A spirit canoe with its crew of ancestral figures. Linden-Museum, Stuttgart.

way through a termites' tunnel and escapes in his canoe to make islands and found other villages.

The posthole murder motif also occurs hundreds of miles away in the Solomon Islands, where it was told to F. E. Fox, but there the two brothers are replaced by a band of brothers, the youngest of whom rushes off as soon as he is born with his umbilical cord slung round his neck. In Malaita he has the fanciful name Delectable Lizard; in San Cristobal he is impressively called Warohunugamwanehaora.

As soon as he is born he rushes off to see his brothers who are building a canoe house. On his way he notices the shadow of a dog with its ears pricked. He arrives just as his brothers are struggling to balance the ridge pole on the upright main posts, and suggests that it will balance better if they carve the tops of the main posts so that they resemble the shape of the shadow of the dog's head. His brothers take his advice but they resent his precocity. When he uproots a tree and simply thrusts it into the ground as a house-post they can stand no more and decide to kill him. They invite him to enlarge the size of a posthole, and when he climbs in they ram the post down on him. Suddenly they hear a voice above them saying 'That's right. Let it down carefully, now!' And they see the aggravating boy perched on the top of the post.

In later attempts to kill him they expose him to many dangers including a giant clam, a man-eating fish and a great boar but when they get home they always find he has arrived before them and is seated in front of the canoe house waiting for them. At last his patience is exhausted, and as an example to the others he cooks the eldest brother and they all eat him.

In many parts of Melanesia a human life or head was indeed required for enterprises like house-building or the launching of a canoe. Amongst the Kiwai Papuans, for example, few visitors would voluntarily have entered a new ceremonial house unless they were certain that blood had already been shed. The

Right In south Malekula figures to commemorate the dead, called Rambaramb, were made of vegetable paste applied to a base of tree fern and painted. The limbs were made of rolled banana leaf and the face moulded over a skull. A wig was made from spider's web. The feathers, ornaments, and objects such as heads from the Nevinbür dancing sticks that were attached to extensions from the shoulders, all indicated a man's rank. (*See* p. 93.) Australian Museum, Sydney.

Opposite A double Nevinbür effigy. Australian Museum, Sydney.

choice of a stranger was natural because a stranger's death was less likely to cause ill-feeling in the community.

The Band of Brothers

In Vanuatu the antagonism between two brothers is extended to rivalry among a number of brothers. Usually one of these brothers, either the eldest or the youngest, has a creative role but frequently he is thwarted by the stupidity or evil intent of one or all of them. In many other stories the emphasis is placed on his tricky behaviour or the element of conflict. The most famous of these bands of brothers is most certainly Qat and his eleven brothers all called Tangaro, who are from the Banks Islands. Many regard Qat as the counterpart of Polynesian Maui; but Maui himself appears in the islands of southern Vanuatu. On Aniwa he is Matshiktshiki, on Efate Maui-tukituki, on Erronan Amoshashiki, and on the Polynesian outlyer of Santa Cruz he is Mosigsig. The only feat which these heroes share with their Polynesian namesake is land-fishing. All their other activities are typically Melanesian, including the defeat of ogres and the release of the sea.

Similarly Qat's personality is fundamentally Melanesian. He fishes up land like Maui but in many ways he is closer to Nareau of Micronesia, especially when he plays the trickster. Like Nareau he has a companion, Marawa, who takes the form of a spider. On the island of Santa Maria in the Banks Islands Marawa countered Qat's life-giving activities by

making death. Qat shaped men and women from dracaena wood and 'beguiled them into life' by dancing and beating a drum. Marawa did the same, but when his figures began to move he buried them in a deep pit. After seven days he dug up the lifeless rotting bodies and since then men have died.

On the other hand the people of Mota told R. H. Codrington that Marawa was a wood sprite. In the first instance he replaced the chips of a tree which Qat was cutting down to make a canoe. Qat hid behind a chip and caught him – shades here of the Polynesian Rata. Then Marawa turned to and helped Qat build the canoe and afterwards acted as his protector. He rescued Qat from the land-crab's hole in which his wicked brothers had tried to crush him – shades of the attempted posthole murder – and when Qat was trapped in a stretching tree he extended his white hair as a ladder.

Sea voyagers appeal to Qat and Marawa:

'Let the canoe turn into a whale, a
   flying fish, an eagle:
Let it leap on and on over the waves,
Let it go, let it pass out to my land.'

Qat has many associations with the sea and like another seafaring hero from the Trobriands he built a great canoe inland far from the sea. The Trobriander's canoe flew but Qat's tore a channel for itself to the shore and he departed, apparently forever, with many of the good things of the island. The first white men encountered were instantly recognised as the returning Qat and his companions. Although there are other views about his ultimate fate there is almost universal agreement that he came into existence on the island of Vanua Lava when his mother, a stone, burst asunder. The stump of the tree cut for his canoe still stands there and many features of the landscape bear the marks of his passing. As well as having created lands, trees, rocks, pigs and men he is also said to have made women in the same way as the tall hats are made for the Qatu ceremonies; that is by making a frame of rods and rings covered with swathes of sago palm.

A favourite story about Qat describes how he made night because his brothers were tired of perpetual daylight. First he visited I Qong, Night, and returned with the necessary equipment, then he taught his brothers how to sleep and when the cocks crowed and the birds twittered he took a piece of red obsidian and cut through Night, making the dawn.

In most of Vanuatu similar adventures were attributed to Tangaro (Tahar, Taharo, Takaro, Takaru). On some islands Tangaro had no brothers, only a contrary companion called Suqematua. In others he had ten or twelve brothers and the maverick Suqe as well. Very often he had the status of a deity. On the small island of Malo as Takaru, the ruler of the sky world, he mirrored his Polynesian namesake the great god Tangaroa.

The Sky-maiden

Both Tangaro and Qat steal their wives in the classical manner of the 'swan maiden' stories. Qat came upon a group of sky maidens bathing and hid one pair of wings so that one girl had to remain behind. One day Qat's mother reproached her daughter-in-law and the girl wept. Her tears washed away the earth covering her wings and she put them on and flew away. Qat shot an arrow-chain into the sky down which a banyan root wound, and climbed after her into the sky world. He met a man hoeing a garden and begged him not to disturb the root until he was safely down again, but as he descended with his wife the root snapped and he plunged to his death, while she flew to safety.

In Melanesia this 'swan maiden' theme is found only in parts of western and northern New Guinea, New Caledonia and the New Hebrides and this scattered distribution suggests that it has been absorbed independently in each place from outside the area. In the Tangaro story the maiden's name Vinmara resembles the popular Malaysian name for the sky maiden, Widadari.

Right A figure from Mala or Ulawa in the Solomon Islands. The decoration is inlaid mother of pearl. British Museum.

Opposite Crocodile carvings on house post of ceremonial house at Kanganaman, on the Sepik River, New Guinea. Once exclusively for men, it is now a national monument, and open to all.

This in turn stems from the Sanskrit *Vindhyadara*.

In an Arapesh story, again recorded by Margaret Mead, the 'swan' is an earthbound cassowary. Before she bathed she removed, not her wings but her 'apron' – the tuft of feathers on the cassowary's hindquarters – and this was stolen and hidden in the rafters. She recovered her garment when an insect disturbed the bundle and a piece fell in front of her – a detail which reflects Micronesian influence. This is also evident in another story from Santo, Vanuatu, in which the great sky deity Yetar is described as the child of a 'fish woman'. When he cries his father teases the mother by saying 'the son of a fish is crying', so she carries him off in a huff.

An example from the southern island of Efate provides a link with the Polynesian story of Tawhaki and Kariki, for the children of Tagaro and the sky woman are called Maka Tafaki and Karisi Bum and when they seek their mother in the sky world they, like their Polynesian namesakes, encounter their old blind grandmother who is counting yams for her cooking pot.

Fabulous Inventors and Innovators

The myths of the tribes of the Papuan Gulf and their neighbours the Torres Strait Islanders feature innumerable culture heroes each of whom was concerned with only a limited aspect of creation or the introduction of a

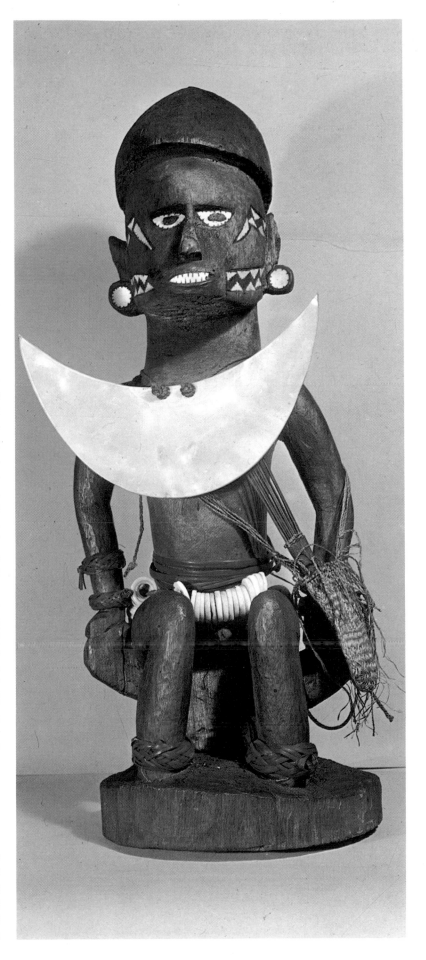

few particular things. Together they brought new foods, taught men how to garden and to perform garden magic; how to hunt, catch turtle by using sucker fish, use wooden charms to increase fish yields, and how to make houses, fish traps, masks and drums. They inaugurated trade, initiation ceremonies, rites for the dead, ceremonies for the increase of men and their food supply, and ritual for success in war. Moreover almost every feature of the landscape reminded men that these powerful predecessors had once dwelt in their country or passed by. Many of these

exploits were recounted to G. Landtman by the Kiwai Papuans.

One of the great heroes of the Kiwai Papuans was Marunogere. Before he taught them how to build their great communal houses – some exceed 300 feet (91 metres) in length – they lived in miserable holes in the ground. As soon as the first ceremonial house was built he inaugurated it with a moguru or life-giving ceremony, which also aimed at making men great fighters. Although he tried several different cult objects in turn – a bundle of arrows, a bunch of coconuts and a string of fish – the

men were still beaten. So he sought a more effective object, and formed a pig out of a lump of sago, making its hair, tail and features out of the fibre and shell of the coconut. The pig ran off into the bush and Marunogere sent men to catch it alive for the ceremony. Just as his dogs cornered the animal his son's arrow killed it. The father was very angry because this not only meant that he would die but also that henceforth all men would die. However his ritual with the dead pig did make the men great warriors and it was re-enacted yearly in the moguru when young boys

crawled over the corpse of a wild boar decked out in the finery of a fighter. Marunogere also bored a hole in each woman to give her sexual organs, and in the evening he was content to die after he felt the gentle rocking of the great house as the men and women were locked in the first sexual embrace. This part of the myth provided the sanction for the ritual initiation, during the moguru, of the young boys and girls into adult sexual life.

The 'strengthening' of the young Kiwaian males was continued in the Mimia ceremonies which included

mock fights with flaming torches. These took place when the sweet-tasting mimia reed was in season. The wild woman Abere – a notorious seducer and slayer of men – and her girl companions were loosely associated with this ceremonial cycle. It was claimed that the reed grew up round Abere to hide her from one of her victims. Her girl companions sometimes lent their names to the wooden figures worn by the participants in the ceremonies. The story of Abere and her girls is bound up with that of Mesede the great marksman whose bow caused spontaneous fire when it

Above When the interior of the great *diama* or men's clubhouse at Urama, Papuan Gulf, New Guinea, was photographed by Frank Hurley in 1921, the great masks used in initiation ceremonies still hung there. On the right is a skull rack, and below it is a line of *gope* or ancestral tablets, above a row of pig skulls. These boards which are imbued with spiritual power stand at the entrance to each clan cubicle. Their powers included the ability to ward off sickness and other dangers, and early European visitors were greeted by men waving *gope*.

Opposite A main house post of the ceremonial house at Kanganaman on the Sepik River, New Guinea, showing the way in which the top is shaped to support the curved surface of the horizontal beam which rests on it. The carving probably represents a wood spirit.

was drawn. He rescued Abere's son from a crocodile and afterwards seized her girls. His wife was jealous and had them killed and the headless body of the youngest and most beautiful was thrown into the sea. It became hard like a log and was washed ashore. The flies hollowed it out and another hero, Morave, covered one end with skin and used it as a drum. This was the prototype of the Dibiri drum which is waisted like a human body.

Many of the adventures of the great hero Sido (Hido, Iko) who is known to all the tribes of the gulf district as the first man to do many things, are concerned with his wanderings as a spirit after death. The Kiwaians say he courted and won the beautiful Sagaru only to lose her to a rival whose powerful magic carried her away on a stretching tree. The two men fought and Sido was killed, but flying foxes, bats and entangling creepers barred his way to the land of the dead and compelled him to wander on earth. He got up to many shameful tricks, including molesting women and children, until one day, in the shape of a seashell, he was swallowed by a woman who was joined back to back with another. He was born again and cut the women apart. Once again he tried to evade death by changing his skin but he was observed by two children and died.

The women buried his body, keeping his skull. His spirit wandered westward and wherever he paused the dead now pause on the way to Adiri, the land of the dead. His mothers caught up with him by a well on Boigu Island and gave him a drink from his own skull, thus preventing him from returning to life. When he reached Adiri he planted gardens to feed the dead. Then he turned himself into a great pig and split his belly open so that his backbone formed the roof and his sides the walls of a great house. This act was commemorated in the Kiwaian practice of fastening the parts of a pig to the framework of a house – the vertebrae were attached here and there along the ridge spars and the jaw was placed under the threshold – so that the house

Left Small flat wooden boards called *mimia* were hung round the necks of the participants in the Mimia ceremonies performed by the Kiwai to strengthen the young men. Similar life-size boards were ranged at the sides of the centre aisle of the ceremonial house during the ceremony. They were also carried in the canoes of raiding parties so that the power with which they were saturated could support the enterprise. Museum of Mankind, London.
Opposite A mask from the Torres Straits island of Saibai. Carved from wild-plum wood, it was worn at a festival for the gathering of wild plums. Royal Scottish Museum, Edinburgh.

suggested the body of a great pig.

The Cambridge Expedition led by A. C. Haddon to the Torres Straits Islands collected stories about a number of truly terrible island wanderers associated with cults of war involving headhunting, cannibalism, and sexual abuses. There were the Brethren, one of whom was Malu who settled on Mer in the Murray Islands. After travelling there as a man with a shark's head he turned into a shark. His famous drums, Wasikor and Nemau were used in the Malu ceremonies. The smallest of the Murray Islands, Waier, provided a home for the cult of another fierce warrior Waiet who travelled there on a feather.

Kwoiam, the murderer of Mabuiag, whose story is also known to the Kiwai, was said to have had the straight hair and 'the wild throat and half-wild heart' of an Australian mainlander. He has been identified with Siverri, the culture hero of the Tjungundji of the Cape York peninsula, who say Siverri went north to Mabuiag and was killed. However there are many things about him – his typically Papuan crescent-shaped pearl shell ornaments, his cylindrical drum and his head-hunting activities – which suggest that he has a Papuan origin.

Kwoiam was an ugly child and a bully. One day he lifted a loop of his blind mother's plaiting with his toe and she cursed whoever walked there. He retaliated by first killing her and then murdering the rest of the family. He wreathed her severed head with coconut leaves and he painted and

This Torres Straits dancing mask of turtle shell in the form of a crocodile with a fishtail was probably worn in a Malu ceremony. Pitt Rivers Museum, Oxford.

decorated the skulls of the men and women in the manner which has been used ever since. Too late he felt sorry for his action and began to kill everybody else to atone for his mother's murder. He lured people from the neighbouring islands and even raided the villages of the New Guinea mainland. On the return journey he cast the skulls and skins into the sea to make reefs and sandbanks. Some say he grew tired of killing and entered the ground on Mabuiag or turned into a stone. Others say his power diminished and the hook of his throwing stick broke. He retreated uphill and was killed. His weapons were thrown back to mainland Australia by the islanders who declared: 'That style of killing must stay there.'

The story of old Tamatu of Paraoka (Irian) who introduced the forging of iron, is completely within the tradition of the wandering hero. He had such great power that he could make mountains and kick them into nothingness again. He planted sago and it grew at once. As he travelled westward performing wonders, chopping down forests and burning the wood, presumably as fuel for his furnace, he taught men to make metal axes, lances, harpoon heads and knives. When his pupils forgot the

practical lessons, he gave them iron filings in water to drink and sang and beat the drum until they remembered. Some could not stand the loud noise so they drove him away shouting: 'Go away bald pate, shining coconut shell, bald head.' At last he picked up a stone and placed it on his head and petrified. His wives seated themselves back to back and did the same thing.

Fate of the Soul after Death

In some parts of Melanesia, particularly the Trobriands, the southern and central Solomon Islands, the Banks Islands and northern Vanuatu, there is a belief in dual souls, one of which goes to an afterworld usually situated either on an island or underground while the other takes various forms. In parts of the Solomon Islands it passes into sharks, fish, birds, animals, men, stones and trees and as a person ages his companions watch for a creature that by its persistent association with him reveals itself as his future incarnation. Sometimes the head of a man is placed in a hollow wooden shark and floated in the sea. Then the soul passes into the first sea creature that approaches it.

The route taken by the souls of the

dead to the afterworld is usually well defined. The Fijians believed that this Spirit Path was hazardous and had many stopping places, so that only the warrior who died a violent death was likely to complete the journey. Not all areas have elaborate spirit itineraries but most believe in a guardian at the entrance who challenges the credentials of the newcomers. If an islander from Ysabel in the Solomons does not bear the mark of a frigate bird on the palm of his hand, he is tossed to oblivion. If a spirit from Aurora in Vanuatu does not belong to the graded society or Sukwe, he is as nothing and hangs like a flying fox upon a tree. Those south-east Solomon Islanders who go to the afterworld, Marapa, believe common and idle people become white ants' nests and serve as food for the more vigorous souls of influential

Above This is a small model of a figure of the Torres Straits culture hero, Waiet, which stood in a cave high on the rock face of the island of Waier, Murray Islands. Part of the headdress is missing. The Murray Islanders claim that Walot came from Mabuiag and introduced the spirit pantomimes, using animal masks. In the west he was associated with funerary ceremonies, but in the Murray Islands his cult was concerned with fertility. In the western islands they tell a story of how another culture hero taught him to beat the drum and he stole a famous mask. University Museum of Archaeology and Anthropology, Cambridge.

Left Figure of a woman, from the Lower Fly River, Papuan Gulf, New Guinea. It was probably associated with the Moguru ceremonies. Field Museum of Natural History, Chicago, Illinois.

Above The *korwar* figures from Geelvink Bay in Irian Jaya (New Guinea) were carved when death occurred. Sometimes the outsize head was hollowed out to take the skull which was believed to retain the essence of spiritual power of the person. The spirit was thought to inhabit the figure and its help was invoked in times of danger or illness. Often an intermediary held the head and was possessed by the spirit who spoke through him. The snake motif is common in this area and the decorative style reflects a contact with a culture with a knowledge of metal-work. Museum für Völkerkunde, Basel.

Opposite Squatting figure from Bougainville Island in the Solomons, representing a protective spirit and probably used as a prow ornament. In this region the bulging forehead and prominent jaw are characteristic of male figures. Museum für Völkerkunde, Basel.

men. When at last men forget them, these too turn into white ants' nests. So the fate of a man's soul depends not only on his own conduct but also on the care with which his relatives carry out the necessary funerary rites.

To make matters more confusing those souls that go to an afterworld can also return as ghosts in human or animal form. In many places their return is institutionalised in annual ceremonies like the Tamate of the Banks Islands or the Horiomu or ghost pantomimes of the Kiwai. On the other hand many of the masked pageants of Melanesia, like those of the Elema of the eastern Papuan Gulf, represent the visitation not of ancestral spirits but of spirits of the sea and bush. These spirits who have never been human can also take the shape of every kind of creature especially sharks, crocodiles, snakes, turtles and cassowaries, so that the difference between human and non-human spirits is often ill-defined. There are many myths which explore the Melanesian's success or failure in coming to terms with this teeming spirit world.

Spirits that Help and Spirits that Hinder

Very often esoteric knowledge and paraphernalia such as masks, head-dresses, bullroarers were acquired from a spirit, ancestral or otherwise. The Arapesh tell how some men heard marvellous music coming from a lake. One jumped in and followed a root to the underworld where his ancestress gave him the sacred triple flutes and the hour-glass hand-drum, with the warning that they must not be played for two months. When the ghosts discovered their loss they haunted the outskirts of the villages until they heard the music of the flutes and then they joined the festival and persuaded the men to let them play. As soon as the ghosts took hold of the instruments they sank back into the ground with them. At once the men set about carving new ones of the same design.

Many of the myths about spirit

helpers expose the dominant tensions of the societies where they are told. In eastern Melanesia power, prestige and social status depend on the progressive accumulation of wealth in the form of garden produce, pigs and money and upon its effective distribution as payments for service, feasts and gifts. In the Banks Islands this process is institutionalised in the practice of buying admission to, and promotion in, the graded society or Suque. To begin a man must have a proposer, usually his mother's brother, to whom he gives a pig. His patron then gives a feast at which he receives money and presents from the candidate and the guests; so the ball starts rolling. In such a competitive set-up a man without relatives or wealth is at a considerable disadvantage, so myths about poor orphans who have supernatural helpers are irresistible fantasies.

In the story about Ganviviris from Mota, told to R. H. Codrington, a sea spirit provided him with enough money to buy the produce of several gardens for a feast so that in one day he bought two grades in the Suque. The spirit's name was Ro Som (money). Ganviviris continued to advance himself every five days by buying entrance to each successive grade with prize pigs whose tusks had grown full circle. Not satisfied with this he determined to join other Suque, including one that Ro Som specifically forbade him to attempt. While the feast was in progress the people were amazed to see a woman appear wearing magnificent bracelets and a boar's tusk on her right arm. Her face was smeared with red earth and pigs' tails were fastened in her hair. She entered the young man's house, but when they followed her they found nobody there and his money bags were empty and his pigs gone. As he no longer had property to distribute his claims lapsed and after five days he died.

For the Melanesian, the bush and sea around him are made dangerous by a great variety of supernatural emanations. There are special ghosts like those of beheaded men whose wounds glow in the dark, or like the

Above Tamate mask, New Hebrides. Said to have been worn on the day new members of the *tamate* society emerged after thirty days' seclusion. *Tamate* means ghost and the uninitiated thought the wearers were ghosts. University Museum of Archaeology and Anthropology, Cambridge.

Right Carved and inlaid figure of a shark-headed man, probably a canoe prow ornament, from the Solomon Islands. Sharks and other fish played a prominent part in the myths and beliefs of the islanders; in the Solomons it was believed that the souls of men, particularly successful bonito fishermen, were reincarnated in sharks. On Ulawa sharks were regarded as the guardians of schools of bonito, and each landing stage on the island had its own guardian shark. University Museum of Archaeology and Anthropology, Cambridge.

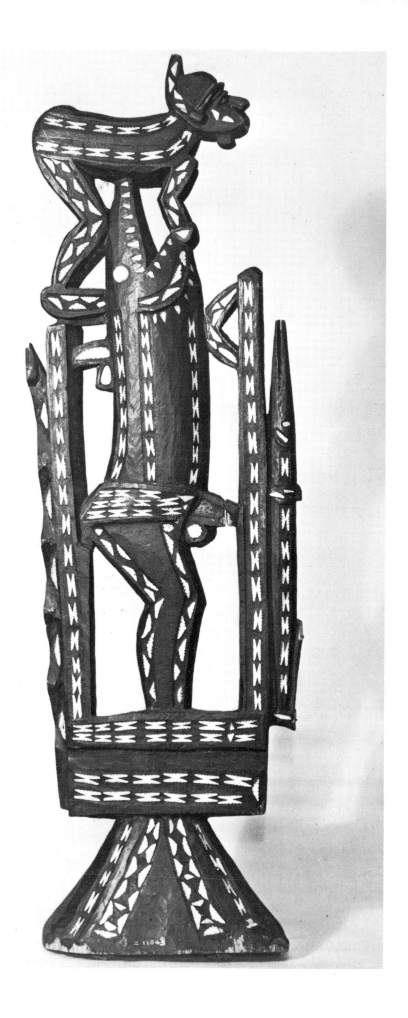

Above This female figure was carved in tree fern to mark a man's attainment of the *lon bul* grade (a high grade) in the social hierarchy of south-east Ambrim in the New Hebrides. Staatliches Museum für Völkerkunde, Hamburg.

Above The Elema have a spectacular cycle of ceremonies that extend over many years called *Hevehe*, in honour of the sea spirits who are said to inhabit Orokolo Bay in the Papuan Gulf. At one of these ceremonies of the installation of the doors of a new ceremonial house, light-hearted dances are performed and a special type of mask, the *eharo*, is worn. Sometimes they represent mythical beings, and sometimes models of totemic creatures surmount the masks themselves. (*See* p. 90.) Pitt Rivers Museum, Oxford.

gesges of New Ireland who are the ghosts of unborn children of women who die in pregnancy. There are also the spirit doubles of living men. In New Ireland they say that when a man dies his *gas* or double dies too. A man called Muk once came across a group of them, and he mistook them for his friends until he noticed one in his own image. They befriended him and helped him to catch fish. Later they heard him telling other men about the encounter and immediately strangled him. Now *gas* remain invisible. The mountain Kukukukus of New Guinea tell how a boy was approached by a spirit with the face of his mother's brother, who pierced his nose septum and inserted a bush fowl's bone. His real uncle found him and took him home. It was noticed soon after that he had become a great fighter, so henceforth initiation included the nose-piercing ceremony.

Amongst the many classes of spirits

Above Dressed in a tunic of spider's web, with artificial arms and hands attached, this dancer appears as a *temes at im buritian*, or ghost in a performance for a high grade in the *nawalan* society, Malekula, Vanuatu. Men could advance themselves through the various grades by making payment in pigs. Photographed by A. B. Deacon in the late 1920s.

Opposite A sea adaro, or spirit, represented in a wood-carving from San Cristobal in the Solomon Islands. Museum of Mankind, London.

tattooing is beyond the normal skill and in Vanuatu they use too much lime to bleach their hair. Their joints are usually reversed and sometimes their heads are too. In their own shape they are gross and ugly and sometimes have exceedingly large ears. The Torres Straits Islanders call them *dogai* and place their effigies on their canoe prows. Once a man was digging for eggs in a bush hen's mound and mistakenly seized some cowrie shells attached to a dogai sleeping there. Off he ran with the dogai in pursuit and the village in turmoil. When he shot her they turned on him and killed him too. They were both transformed into stars and the chase continues across the heavens.

There is another strange man-beast who has ears like pandanus leaf umbrellas one of which he lies on and the other he wraps round himself. The Kiwaians call him an Origoruso and say he came from underground. In Ulawa in the Solomons he is called Siho i Salo according to W. G. Ivens, and is said to have come from the sky in a shower of rain. He settled himself next to two fishermen, swallowing everything they caught. At length they left him on the pretext that they were going to fetch more bait. After a while he realised he had been tricked and ambled off after them to the canoe house where all the men were gathered trying to decide what to do about him. Once again he settled himself down and ate everything. Eventually a great sorcerer, Porotaki, cast a spell and Siho unfolded his great ears and went to sleep. While he slept the men escaped and blocked the path to the village. Siho awoke and after searching fruitlessly for his intended victims he trundled off. He came to Porotaki's garden and pulled down the vines to make a nest. Porotaki dreamed that he was there and visited the garden. He fed the brute raw pig-meat and made a bargain with him that he should remain to protect the garden from ghosts. From that time on this was Siho's role.

This may seem a trivial tale but it is important because the monstrous Siho has travelled a long way to

of non-human origin are the sea *adaro* or sprites of the south-east Solomon Islands who travel in water-spouts or sunshowers and use rainbows as bridges. They are partly human and partly fishlike in appearance. They shoot men with flying fish, and when their missile strikes, the victim feels pain in the nape of his neck and loses consciousness. He may recover if an offering of a flying fox is made in time. The chief of these sprites is Ngorieru who haunts the sea-shore off the coast of San Cristobal. Passing canoe crews dip their paddles quietly and speak in low tones lest they attract his attention. Sea sprites also visit men in their dreams and teach them new songs and dances.

Another special class of spirit is the changeling – usually female – who is the central character in some of the more amusing *horror* stories of the area. Her favourite trick is to impersonate a man's wife and seduce him. These changelings can usually be detected because they tend to overdo things; in the Banks Islands their

Above In Melanesia the purpose of carving things in everyday use is principally to enchance the object but the decorative designs chosen are usually those of plants and animals which may represent one of several things: a clan emblem, a totem or a animal form taken either by spirits who were once men, or spirits of non-human origin. They may not be direct representations but the underlying symbolism is clear. The crocodile head canoe prow is from the Middle Sepik region, New Guinea.

Right A representation of an ancestral spirit, modelled in clay on a vegetable fibre base. Such figures were carried on staves by ceremonial dancers. The spirit was actually believed to be present in the figure on such occasions. From Ambrim in the New Hebrides.

Melanesia. A spirit with his form is also known to the Naga tribesmen of northern India who share other cultural traits with the Oceanians. Moreover he personifies those vague malignant forces which harass and obstruct man rather than harm him. The events of the story – beginning with the relentless pursuit of the men by Siho and culminating in his being tamed and enlisted as a protector of gardens – emphasise the dual nature of supernatural forces which are so powerful that they are potentially dangerous to man and yet, given the right magic, can be controlled for the benefit of man, particularly for the productivity of his gardens.

Above In the western islands of the Torres Straits Dogai was thought to be a female malignant spirit. In the eastern islands it seems to have been a male, having the power to blight coconuts, destroy fish and cause high tides. It was associated with a bright star, probably Mars. In September and October a *dogaira* ceremony was held in which a mask like this one was worn. The purpose seems to have been either as a thanksgiving for a good yield in the gardens or in order to secure one. Offerings were hung in the branches of nearby large trees and piled underneath. University Museum of Archaeology and Anthropology, Cambridge.

Left The small double figure of a local deity set on the platform of a hook carved from whale ivory has a fascinating history. It was part of the collection of Sir Arthur Gordon, later Lord Stanmore, who was Governor of Fiji in the eighteen-seventies. It is said that the image came originally from Tonga and that it was given by the chief of Sabeto (Fiji) to a Fijian 'doctor' as a fee for curing a swollen neck. The 'doctor' returned with it to his own district, Nandi on Viti Levu, where the image became possessed by a goddess called Lilavatu, wife of the chief god of Nandi. The 'doctor' built a temple for her and he and his heirs became her priests. It is said that a thin squeaky voice came from the image. She was a dangerous goddess who could cause swollen necks. If people failed to make offerings to her they died or were killed in war. Lila was the name given by Fijians to an epidemic which arrived with the first European ships. University Museum of Archaeology and Anthropology, Cambridge.

Australia

The Bond between Man and Nature

The fading image of the Spirit of the Long Grass, Morkul-kua-luan, can be seen on a rocky outcrop near the boundary of the Agricultural Research Station at Katherine, Northern Territory. He is shown with his eyelids half-closed to protect his eyes from the prickling grass-seeds as he moved through the wild grain. His beak-like nose resembles the sharp sheath of the seed. His presence there on the rock was intended to ensure a plentiful and recurring supply of the stands of native sorghum which grow in the area, for although the local Aborigines made no attempt to cultivate this grain they gathered it and pounded it into a meal called morkul, to make a nourishing food.

The proximity of Morkul to the research station underlines the contrast between White Australia's technological approach to land and the Aborigine's intimate and intricate adaptation over the centuries to nature's cycle. The occupancy of Australia is now known to have extended so far back in time that as environments changed so must have subsistence patterns and ways of life. The foundation of pre-contact traditional Aboriginal culture, characterised particularly by an elaborate spiritual and ceremonial life, probably dates from 4000 to 3000 years ago. The broad description of Aborigines as semi-nomadic hunter-gatherers inadequately conveys the degree to which their adaptation was one of resource management, dependent on detailed knowledge of habitats and seasonal variations. For instance, extensive stone fish traps

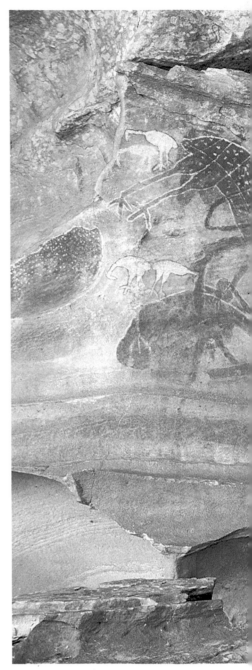

and weirs were made on many inland rivers, and in the marshes of Western Victoria channels were dug to trap eels. Along the coasts base camps of sturdy structures were occupied for several months at a time while the fishing was at its best; people came from hundreds of miles each spring to the Snowy Mountains to catch the succulent Bogong moths and to the stands of Bunya Bunya pines on the south Queensland coast to gather sweet kernels. These occasional gatherings also provided the opportunity for inter-group ceremonies and trade. Australia was covered by a network

of trading chains by which such things as stone axes, ochre and pearlshell travelled for long distances across the continent. The Aborigine's isolation was also tempered by contact with outsiders from New Guinea and Indonesia and cultural traits filtered through the northern coastal areas and along the trading network. The incorporation into east Arnhem Land mortuary rites of the mast-raising ceremony performed by the crews of departing Macassan trepanging praus is one example of this contact which seems to have increased in the few centuries prior to European settlement. It is not clear why gardening techniques were not adopted by the Aborigines – at least by those in contact with gardening neighbours and in an area where plants like yams and indigenous grains grew – but probably the main reason lies in the successfulness of their own subsistence strategies. There were obviously broad regional differences, but whatever the environment – in the desert, along the banks of a river like the Murray or by the sea – for the Aborigine, this success depended on the maintenance of the special bond between himself and

The caves and rock shelters of the sandstone plateaux of Cape York Peninsula are particularly rich in rock art, and the gallery of the White Ibis is one of the liveliest of all. Because there is a permanent water supply 40 metres (131 feet) below the shelter it could have been used as a camp site throughout the year rather than seasonally.

Above The Songman. His song concerns a sacred ceremony to be performed on the next day. It also serves as a warning to the women and the uninitiated to keep away. The clapping stocks mark the rhythm. Liverpool River, Arnhem Land.

Opposite A man of the cockatoo totem is about to take part in a *pukamuni* ceremony, or funeral rite. Melville Island, off the coast of Arnhem Land.

nature, expressed in his beliefs and sustained by his ceremonies.

His desired objective was to achieve not change but predictable regularity; regularity of the seasons and of plant growth and animal increase. He particularly recognised the life-giving properties of rain; though his fear of drought was matched by his fear of floods, storms and tornadoes. He understood the bond between himself and nature to be a totemic one and believed that this relationship had been established in the mythical past or Eternal Dreamtime by the activities of creative beings. Some of these, like the Sky Heroes of eastern Australia, or the Fertility Mothers and their companions of the far north, established the totemic system; others, like the totemic beings of inland Australia, were themselves actually identified with a particular aspect of nature symbolised by an emblem or totem; for example, a cockatoo, a wind, or the honeysuckle. Each of these totemic ancestors was respon-

sible for the laying down of spirit centres, not only for the particular animals and plants with which each was concerned, but also for spirit children. It is these pre-existent spirits which enter the bodies of the women of the group and are born. So a person's cult totem or dreaming is usually related to his origin from a particular spirit centre laid down by a particular totemic ancestor.

Although many of the creative beings of the Dreamtime took human form, they were cast in a gigantic mould and possessed supernormal powers. In this group belong the Sky Heroes of the south east and the Fertility Mothers of Arnhem Land, but the latter sometimes took snake form. The totemic ancestral beings seemed to be able to slip from human to animal form and back again, though sometimes this metamorphosis took place only once.

Like the Aborigines many of these Dreamtime beings were wanderers. They made the landscape, established sacred sites and introduced the ceremonies to be performed there. Their ways led them across tribal and linguistic boundaries, so that each part of a tribe was most knowledgeable about that section of a myth which described events which took place in its territory. However these mythical paths also linked neighbouring groups and they came together for great ceremonial gatherings. One famous site was the honey-ant ceremonial ground at Ljaba in the territory of the northern Aranda in the Macdonnell Ranges of Central Australia.

Some totemic ancestors had dominant roles. For instance, the Tjilpa or native cat ancestors of the Aranda were responsible for establishing, in the proper order, the initiation rites of circumcision, sub-incision (the opening of a certain length of the meatus) and ordeal by fire. But fundamentally this totemic view of life meant that the totemic ancestors shared the labour of creation. This same principle of the division of labour also applies to man's approach to these creative forces. The guardianship of the myths, rites, sacred objects and sites associated with a particular totemic ancestor rests with the members of a particular religious unit who all share the same cult totem, and each of these groups takes its share of the responsibility for ritually ensuring that the life essence created during the Eternal Dreamtime is not only sustained but perpetuated.

They do this in rites in which the actors *become* the beings and re-live their deeds. They also perform increase rites in which the multiplication of a particular natural species may be brought about by actions such as the retouching of rock paintings, regrooving of rock engravings, or the disclosure of sacred objects such as particular stones. The use of blood drawn from the arm or the genital organ is also believed to release the spiritual essence. It may be rubbed on a body or totemic object or used as a fixative for other decorations such as down. It may be scattered over, dripped on, or rubbed into an object. Red ochre may be used in the same way.

Throughout Australia the religious life of the group is controlled by the men but this does not mean that women have no part in it. The degree of actual participation, however, varies from area to area. In some districts women have their own secret ceremonies such as the djarada or love-magic ceremonies of Northern Australia. They may also be involved in the men's ritual from a distance. For instance they may answer ritual calls made by the men on the ceremonial ground or they may be summoned to act as a chorus or to take a limited part in the ceremonies as they do in the Kunapipi fertility cult of the far north. In Arnhem Land the women see the sacred designs on the men's bodies when they return to camp after a ceremony and they hear and know the 'outside' or general camp versions of sacred songs and myths. Even the negative knowledge of knowing what to avoid must be taken into account, for over much of Australia the death penalty was enforced if women infringed the sacred precincts, or mythological paths, or saw the sacred cult objects.

Amongst the Aranda many of the most beautiful water-hole sites were permanently forbidden to the women of the group. Yet an Aranda woman could be a reincarnation of a totemic being and a male relative acted as a proxy for her in the sacred ceremonies. Moreover there are symbolic connotations between women's life and much of the ritual performed by the men, for example the equation of subincision with menstruation.

The young boy also has 'outside' knowledge but his introduction into adult status and the sacred life begins with his separation from the women, usually at puberty. His initiation usually extends over at least three or four years and each stage of his advance is frequently marked by a physical operation. The order and choice of these varies from group to group: there is the extraction of teeth, hair removal, cicatrization and – in most of inland Australia – circumcision, subincision and ordeal by fire. He is also subjected to harsh disci-

pline, food tabus, and periods of seclusion. His instruction includes passive witnessing of ceremonies, limited participation in ritual acts, the revelation to him of sacred objects, visits to sacred stores of objects, and journeys along mythological paths. Throughout his life aboriginal man's degree of participation in the sacred life increases as his role changes from novice to initiator. He expects that certain mortuary ceremonies will be performed after his death to ensure the safe return of his spiritual essence to the spirit home from which it came. Very often this is a totemic water hole site but in central Australia it may be a sacred object and in south-east Australia it was the sky.

The demands of this intense spiritual life are many, involving the memorising of many hundreds of verses as well as the details of myths; dance steps, ritual acts, and a knowledge of totemic emblems and designs. Ceremonial activities may spread over many months of the year and place an economic strain on the

groups involved. In the old days it made irksome the lives of the young hunters who were subject to the authority of the older men who alone could reveal to them the inner truths which sustained all existence.

These myths are, and were, communicated with a variety and richness of artistic endeavour. There is the vigorous imitative totemic dancing, the compulsive rhythm of the clapping sticks, drone pipe (didjeridu) and chanting, and the beautiful imagery of the songs. There are fantastic headdresses like those of the emu 'men' of the Aranda or the strange ground paintings like those the Warumungu, made to re-live the journey of the great snake Wollunqua.

Through the eyes of the Aborigine the Australian landscape becomes a myth evoking one. The broad sinuous reaches of the Ord and Victoria rivers of the north-west were made by the black-headed python who came out of the sea from the direction of Timor and pushed forward, making the

ranges, until he reached the Barkly Tablelands where he passed underground. The meandering course of Coopers Creek was created by a great rock python, transformed into an iridescent rainbow snake. He drew the flood water after him as he moved homeward. He chose his direction of travel by the wind, because he was blind, and when it dropped he paused and a large sheet of water formed. The broadening of the Murray river as it flows into the entrance lake in South Australia was caused by the swishing tail of the primal Murray Cod as he was pursued by the sky hero Ngurunderi. Wuraka's head appeared above the waves as he walked along the ocean floor towards the Coburg Peninsula in the Northern Territory. He was the companion of the mother creator, Imberombera, and his penis was so heavy he slung it round his neck. He grew tired and sat down at a spot marked by Tor Rock which rises conspicuously from the western plateau of Arnhem Land.

The huge monolithic dome of

Ayers Rock in central Australia, which the Pitjantjatjara people call Uluru, is associated with ten different groups of totemic beings. The vertical gutters and potholes of the southern face are the scars of battle between the Kunia or carpet snake-men and the Liru or poisonous snake-men. The stands of desert oak to the south-west represent the young Liru warriors silently moving in to the attack.

Across the western desert roamed the Wadi Gudjara (Wadi Kudjara), the Two Men; one was a white goanna, the other was a black one. Amongst the places they laid down was a solid hill of red ochre formed from the blood they drew from their veins.

Far away on the other side of the continent, in the district of the Wikmunkan on the gulf side of Cape York, there is a sub-tropical haven of plenty where women gather the many different edible shellfish along the shore and men spear fish, dugong and turtle. The sandbanks, reed-swamps and waterlily lagoons are breeding

grounds for every kind of bird. Here the myths of the totemic ancestors who went down into their *auwa* or abodes build up a detailed picture of bountiful nature which is a strong contrast to the harshness of nature revealed in the myths of the desert people. Even the most uninspiring of food plants are celebrated. Miss U. McConnel, who knew these people intimately, retells the story of the Hard Yam Woman and the Arrow-root Man.

They were a married couple who were always bickering about the best place to camp as they searched for food along the river banks. Finally they agreed to separate. Wandering alone, the Hard Yam Woman became ill and dug a hole for herself in a dry place. She slept without moving and on waking she exclaimed: 'I'm hungry. Who will feed me? I must stay hungry!' She had not even the strength to leave the hole to fetch water, finally she sank down altogether saying, 'Just in this way the root will sink down into its hole!'

Above The painting of great serpents on hardboard, in the manner of bark painting, by an unknown artist from Port Keats, is probably inspired by mythological themes of the Murinbata people of the north-west Northern Territory.

Opposite A painting on bark by the artist Bunia, of Groote Eylandt, illustrates a fight between a dingo and a wallaby. The dingo is the victor. The eagle watches from above, and waits for his share.

Meanwhile the Arrowroot Man also grew old and helpless, and crawling along the water's edge to drink he sank down alone. His stick stood up like the stalk of the arrowroot as a sign to men that the arrowroot is to be found there.

As in many other Aboriginal myths the plot is based on a simple domestic situation and the elaborations of the theme serve to explain everyday tasks: in this case how to gather certain foods and how to treat them to make them soft and edible. For all this has been laid down in the Dreamtime.

Not all Wikmunkan myths are confined to the immediate locality. The journeys of Sivri, the Seagull, and Nyungu, the Torres Straits Pigeon, link the district with the islands to the north. Sivri showed his northern affiliations by his possession of a drum and bow and arrow, whereas on the island of Mabuiag in the Torres Straits where he was known as Kwoiam, he was famous for his seagull dances and his spear. Sivri stole Nyungu's daughter and carried her off to Mabuiag which is the destination of the migrating seagulls. Nyungu decided to give chase, but flew on to Papua. Before he left he turned to each of his children and declared:

You folk, conch shells shall be!
Bailer shells you shall become!
Pearlshells you shall become!
Ducks you shall become!
Native companions be!
I go! Better that I should go!
For white pigeons will come with me!

And so his children remained behind to become the ducks and native companions of the sandbanks and the shells of the sea.

Land and Myth Today

This total worldview in which every detail of the landscape was invested with meaning and every living thing, no matter how insignificant, had its place, was completely shattered by the European invasion. Few settlers

Right The end of the ceremony – in this case the *Rom*, a trading and friendship ceremony of Eastern Arnhem Land. The dancer holds a bunch of cockatoo feathers in one hand and his spirit bag in the other. This is carried by every initiated male. Although the contents may be secret, the bag itself is worn publicly. It is sometimes held between the teeth during a ceremony – or a fight – to give a man courage.

Opposite Paintings like these at Wellington Range, may have been done for love magic.

were able or willing to see beyond the image of the Aborigines as nomads with few meagre possessions; they regarded them as being without religion and even language, and their treatment of them ranged from indifference to brutality.

With the destruction of the Aborigine's own society, the predictable outcome of his attraction to white settlements was conflict and ultimately dependence. He did not appreciate that the white man's fences were boundaries not to be crossed and the white man's cattle was forbidden food. For the Aborigine ownership of the land involved guardianship rather than property rights and it therefore included the idea of land-sharing.

Traditionally, when Aborigines of various groups came together to share the abundance of a particular district in a particular season, that bounty has been assured by the owners' (usually the male members of a clan or tribe) performance of ritual duties and avoidances. A share in the resources was sanctioned perhaps by the mythological and ceremonial links between groups, or might flow from marriage or trading relationships, or the location of an individual's conception site (spiritual not biological) outside his own territory. Such social mechanisms obviously involved reciprocity, but the success of sharing also depended on hospitality not being abused. The fact that these mechanism could also validate transfer of ownership or the formation of new groupings became important when dispossession and/or the drift of Aborigines to white

centres gave rise to new groupings focused on pastoral holdings, missions, government stations and settlements. If there were still local 'owners' in those places they sometimes shared their esoteric knowledge with the incomers, and one way or another the new groupings came to assume collective religious trusteeship of the land. The white Australians' failure to recognise the validity of such changes, or the codes which govern land-sharing, has fuelled the Aboriginal Land Rights movement. Some land claims are made on behalf of these new groupings, others, particularly in Arnhem Land and Central Australia, are part of the 'homelands', 'outstations', or 'country camps movement': a movement away from mission and government settlements 'to settle down country' on lands with which the group has deep spiritual affiliations. This is not a back-to-the-land retreat. The Aborigines insist on their entitlement to medical, educational and housing services, but administrators have been slow to provide the necessary support to ensure the viability of these often isolated 'country camps'. Hence the growing insistence by the Aborigines on self-management and control over available financial resources.

Sky Heroes of the South-East

There are many rock galleries of engravings in south-eastern Australia which were sacred sites, which like those found elsewhere in Australia were associated with ceremonies of

Above The spirit beings called *mimi* who live in the rocks of western Arnhem Land are said to eat men, but yams are their staple food. Thus Nurungulngul of Goulburn Island, chose to paint the flower, leaves and root of the yam plant.

Opposite A painting on bark by the artist Kneepad, of Groote Eylandt, illustrates a creation story. The east wind pushes up the morning star and so makes daylight. With the light comes the earth, man, rocks and all other things.

123

123

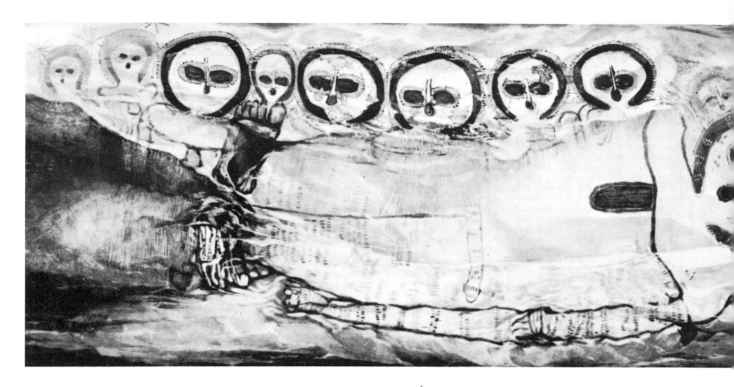

a revelationary and initiatory nature, but only fragments of the sanctioning myths about the great sky heroes they celebrated have survived.

Throughout most of the eastern third of Australia there was a belief in a sky world, the abode of spirit beings who dwelt on earth in the time of the founding drama. The Wotjobaluk of Victoria thought that the sky rested on the earth and prevented the sun from moving until a magpie with a long stick propped it up. Other tribes believed that the sky rested on mountains, or a pine tree, or eucalyptus trees. Some referred to the sky world as a 'gum tree land' or 'the bright bone of the cloud'. It was also thought to be full of quartz crystal, the stone associated with both the rainbow snake and the medicine men.

Some early investigators like Howitt maintained that in the southeast there was also a belief in a dominant spirit being who was revealed to initiates as All-Father, and it seems that the masculine principle of creation was the dominant one in eastern Australia where similar creative activities were attributed to a great sky hero whose name changed from tribe to tribe. In the eastern coastal strip he was known as Dhurramulan and west of the Dividing Range he was called Baiame. In some

Above The great Wondjina lies on his side in the overhanging rock shelter at Wonalirra, near the Chapman River in the northern Kimberley district. Many Wondjina are painted in a horizontal position and the reason often given is that in the Dreamtime the beings entered the shelters to lie down to die; other wondjina fixed their images to the rock face. The legs are separated by a line and the feet are placed at right angles so that the soles are visible. Design traced from the rock face by Dr. K. Lommel. Munich Museum für Völkerkunde.

Right In this preliminary initiation ceremony at Milingimbi in Eastern Arnhem Land the boy is given the red parrot feather armlets which mark the beginning of his change of status. His head and shoulders are draped with gifts of yarn and red parrot feather strings, tipped with white down. His lower trunk and thighs are being rubbed with red ochre to protect and strengthen him.

places Dhurramulan was described as the one-legged son of Baiame. Many Victorian tribes knew him by variations of the name Bunjil and towards the lower Murray River region he was known as Nurrundere, or Ngurunderi.

These creators gave shape to a bare and featureless land. They made the rivers and the hills and added trees and other vegetation. At first there were only animals, birds and reptiles so they made humans — usually out of amorphous beings. Bunjil was

believed to have made two men out of clay while his brother, the Bat, raised women up out of water. These creators also gave men tools and weapons. They laid down the rules and customs by which men should live and introduced initiation ceremonies. In the ceremonies of the Bora ground the sound of the swung bullroarer was the voice of Dhurramulan; initiates were shown a figure of him modelled in relief on the ground. The mouth was filled with quartz crystal; he had a large phallus.

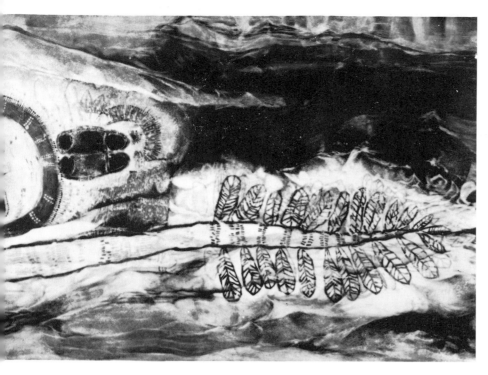

These primal beings chose many different ways to journey to the sky world. One climbed a stretched kangaroo sinew, another was swept thither by a whirlwind. Sometimes, together with the other protagonists in the founding drama, they took their places in the heavens as the sun, moon, or stars, particularly the Pleiades or the Milky Way.

This belief in a sky world and sky beings was also important in the extreme north-west of the continent. It even occurred in inland Australia where it co-existed with the dominant themes of creative totemic ancestors who rose out of the ground. For instance the Aranda believed that two self-existent sky beings, the Numbak-ulla, came down and made men and women out of *Inapatua* or amorphous creatures in which the human form was faintly visible. Much farther north the Murinbata also believed in Spirits who Found Themselves without Fathers, though they did not celebrate them in their cult activities. One of these self-existent spirits who was called Noga-main was a giver of spirit children. Yet in spite of his obvious importance ideas about him were vague. W. E. H. Stanner suggests that there could be an historical explanation for this in that he may belong to an earlier

stratum of ideas; or he might well represent a persistent but undeveloped concept of a supreme or dominant being.

How Gidja the Moon made a Woman

Certain personalised animals and phenomena seem to have been the protagonists in the founding dramas more often than others. For instance, Eaglehawk, Crow, Bat, Moon, Sun are familiar mythical characters in many parts of Australia. The Wotjob-aluk believed that in the beginning there was only one sex and that Ngunung-ngunnut, the Bat, determined to remedy the situation by turning his companion into a woman. This motif turns up again in a myth from the Bloomfield river of northern Queensland told to Miss U. McConnel. Mali the Bat was elder brother to Gidja the Moon and this explained why he flew before him, but it was Gidja who made the first woman. He did this by taking Yalungur the Eaglehawk and castrating him. Then he made a baby out of the bark of the bloodwood and milkwood trees and inserted it into the woman. He was much feared by his fellows but his undoing was

brought about by Kallin-kallin the Chickenhawk who decided that Gidja should be punished for choosing Yalungur who was of the same moiety or social grouping as himself. One day when Gidja was crossing a bridge of lawyer vine Kallin-kallin cut the vine and Gidja fell into the rapids and was swept away. Each time he came to the surface he cried out: 'I am not dead.' At length he reached the seashore and finally he passed into the sky to give men a light at night as the moon. Of course Kallin-kallin took Yalungur as his wife and all was well as they were of opposite moieties.

The Whale and the Starfish

In eastern Australia some of the stories that explain how certain animals got their characteristics often share elements with similar tales from the islands, though the trickster motif is not so strong.

There is a story about a starfish, a koala and a bird, the native companion, who were envious of the whale's canoe. While the starfish deloused the whale's head the others made off in the canoe. When the whale discovered his loss he was very angry; he tore the starfish to shreds and flattened him so that he sank down to the ocean floor. But the starfish had cut the whale so badly that water spurted from his wounds as he gave chase. The koala used his strong arms to row hard and just as they reached the land the native companion trampled the canoe so that it sprang a leak and sank. Now it lies as a stone on the sea-floor at the mouth of Lake Illawarra, New South Wales.

The Muramura

In the Dreamtime the muramura wandered over the lands of the Dieri and the neighbouring territories. Their paths were found from Spencer's Gulf in the south, north to Lake Eyre and north again to south-west Queensland. Indeed two groups of

muramura girls travelled as far as the Gulf of Carpentaria and were finally drawn up into the sky by a long hair cord. One lot became the Pleiades and the others became the stars of Orion's belt. These beliefs resembled those of eastern Australia but many stories about other muramura describe either how they turned to stone or how they changed into animal form and sank into the earth. These ideas are similar to those found amongst their neighbours to the west.

There are also different versions about the origin of man. Some said that the muramura creators made

men by smoothing out the limbs of unformed creatures. Others claimed that the earth opened at Lake Perigundi and the totem animals came out unformed and without sense organs. They lay on the sandhills in the warm sun and gradually grew strong until they stood up as men and scattered over the country.

The muramura, like Dreamtime beings elsewhere, were responsible for introducing initiation rites. Two muramura came from the north and while they hunted one brother dived into the water after a boomerang which had gone astray. He acciden-

tally circumcised himself on its sharp edge. The other brother also wanted to become a 'perfected man', so he did the same thing. Then they travelled about the country saving many initiates from death by introducing the use of the stone knife instead of the firestick for the operation of circumcision. Another myth with an almost identical plot told how two other young muramura were the first to sub-incise themselves. These two still wander the desert caring for lost children and returning them to camp.

It is not surprising to find that these desert people had an apocryphal

myth about the possibility of world destruction by a dust storm. It involved a most important mura-mura, Darana the Rainmaker. On one occasion when he 'sang' the rain water rose first to his knees then to his hips and neck. At last he placed his throwing stick in the ground and the water receded. The desert became carpeted with flowers and the witchetty grubs multiplied. He gathered them in, dried them and packed them into bags which he hung in the trees. Then he went on a journey. In his absence two youths, the Dara-ulu, threw their boomerangs at the bags,

breaking one of them. The dust of the grubs flew far and wide and obscured the sun while the other bags shone with a brightness that could be seen at a great distance. The muramura returned and strangled the Dara-ulu. Darana restored them to life again but the others again strangled them. They became two heart-shaped stones. The Dieri kept these carefully wrapped in feathers and fat and believed that if they were scratched perpetual hunger would result, no matter how much was eaten. If they were destroyed, they said, the red dust would cover the earth and all

Above One of the galleries in the Quinkan cave complex, Cape York, in which the male figures in their rayed headdresses suggesting feathers represent culture heroes or ancestral beings, and dance the dingo dance.

Top The most important witchetty grub totemic site of the Aranda tribe was at Underga or Emily's Gap, a gorge in the Macdonnell Ranges, Central Australia. The abstract paintings on the rock face represent the spot where the women of the Dreamtime painted themselves and stood looking up at the witchetty grub men while they performed a sacred ceremony.

Opposite Ayers Rock is an important totemic site for the people of this part of central Australia, who call it Uluru. They say that it rose out of a large flat sandhill.

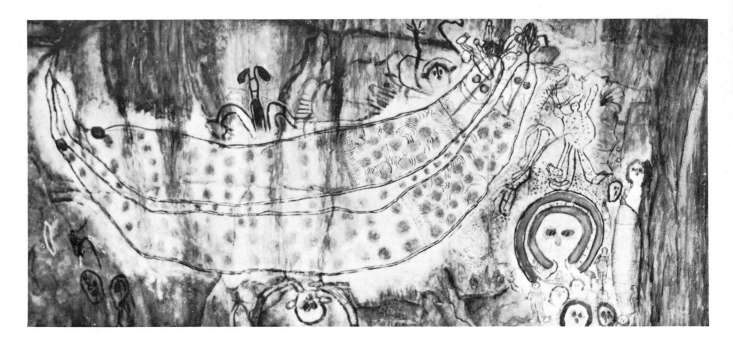

would die in terror. At rainmaking ceremonies these stones are reverently smeared with fat and their songs are sung.

All-powerful Fathers of the Aranda

Several of the Aranda totemic ancestors had more dominant roles than the rest. There were the two culture-bearing Euro brothers who invented the spear and the spearthrower and also taught the art of cooking on hot coals. Then there were the Lakabara or hawk-men who came from the north, and instituted the rite of circumcision and the four-section system of social grouping, and the Tjilpa or native cat-men who came from the south and introduced the further rite of sub-incision.

Most of these totemic ancestors were 'all-powerful fathers', especially amongst the strongly patrilineal northern Aranda, and in his analysis of Aranda myths T. G. H. Strehlow has revealed how strongly the masculine principle of creation is expressed in Aranda thought. In *Aranda Tradition* he retells how the primal ancestor of the witchetty grub totemic group is said to have rested, without moving, in a state between sleeping and waking for countless ages at the foot of a witchetty tree. While he lay

there the grubs swarmed over his body. Occasionally he brushed some gently aside but they returned and crept about him, and bored into him. Time passed. Then one night something fell from his armpit, and taking human shape grew rapidly. The father woke – but only for a moment – to see his first-born son. Then he slept again and produced many other sons in the same way. These young men dug the grubs out of the roots, roasted them and ate them. They also changed into grubs and back again into men. Then one day a stranger came. He was a witchetty grub ancestor from another centre, and he wanted to exchange some of his thin grubs for the fat grubs of Lukara. When his request was refused he stole a bundle and ran off. The sleeping father instantly felt the loss as a sharp pain in his body. He rose and stumbled after the thief but after taking only a few steps he sank down. His body became a living tjurunga and so did the bodies of all his sons. It was these tjurunga that thenceforth contained the living essence of things classed as witchetty grub, whether animal or human. It is this life force which enters a woman as a spirit child and it is this life force which can be tapped by ritual handling of a tjurunga or any other sacred object which represents the totemic ancestor.

The attribution of the procreative act to man without the assistance of woman is a recurring theme in Aranda myths. In many of these the father-son relationship has strong Oedipal connotations for the father is frequently described as being physically handicapped, lame or blind, and very often his injury or death has been caused by his son. Strehlow has recorded the northern Aranda myth which tells how the native cat ancestors introduced the initiation rite of sub-incision. At the end of the ceremony the initiated sons danced round the old Namatjirea for the last time, then they stripped the ceremonial objects and destroyed the ground. The eldest son cast a spell which destroyed his father's sight, and they left him, a pitiful half-wit, alone on the ceremonial ground. The motive given for the young man's action was that the old man refused him equal status in the ceremonies. In reality the admission of young Aranda men to the group's secret life depended on their willingness to submit to the harsh disciplines enforced by the older men.

The Mamandabari of the Warlpiri

The Warlpiri inhabit a desert region which lies to the west of the north-

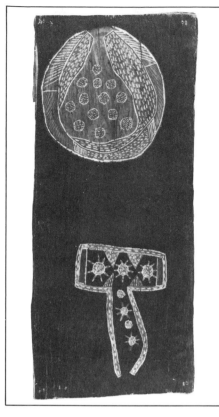

south road in the central section of the Northern Territory. Their most important Dreamtime spirits are the two wanderers, the Mamandabari. They are either referred to as two brothers or as father and son. They rose out of the ground in the north and began to travel south across Warlpiri country, sometimes flying above ground and sometimes travelling under it. They made bullroarers and instituted an important complex of revelationary ceremonies. These included sub-incision and a ceremony involving the digging of pits, the erection of poles and the use of firebrands: all elements to be found in the fertility cults practised by the tribes to the north.

As they journeyed they sang of other dreamings they encountered: the ibis, the rain, the whistling duck, the galah parrots and the stinging red ants. They passed the yellow ochre deposits formed by the falling feathers of the budgerigars, and they came to the red ochre deposits made by falling red galah feathers. When they passed into southern Warlpiri country they ceased to perform their ritual, so it is not yet practised by the people of that district. At last they reached the spinifex country beyond Haast Bluff where their legs were so badly cut by the coarse desert grass that they decided to return home. They travelled mostly underground until they neared their own territory and then, although they were almost exhausted, they resumed their ritual performances wherever they stopped. At last they saw distant campfires burning and thought friends were at hand. Alas, they were the fires of the wild dog-men who pursued and overtook the heroes and destroyed them. Their hearts fell as stones by a water-hole and the dingoes built a fire over their victims' torn bodies to hide the fearful evidence; then they silently loped away. The little budgerigar had been attracted by the terrible commotion and had witnessed the slaughter; he mourned his friends and travelled about the country telling others of their fate.

This myth, recorded by the anthropologist M. J. Meggitt, provides an example of the way in which ideas are diffused, and elements from different sources coalesce. For these male totemic ancestors, so typical of the desert region, are said to have introduced the ritual of the fertility cults like the Kunapipi practised farther north. Indeed, the name given to the cult they sanction is Gadjari, meaning Senior Woman, and the bullroarers which are swung are given the same name.

The Wondjina

In the northern Kimberley district of north-western Australia the primal beings of the Ungud (Dreamtime) were called Wondjina. One such was Warana the Eaglehawk who left two eggs in a nest and went kangaroo hunting. While he was away the eggs were stolen by Wodoi, the Rock Pigeon. Warana guessed who the thief was and gave chase but the pigeon's friend, the owl Djunggun, killed him with his throwing stick and boomerang. Warana turned into a rock painting and the two eggs became two stones outside the cave. Another Wondjina, Walangada, was a being of undefined form. His name means 'belonging to the sky' and he went up there and became the Milky Way. More usually, Aborigines say, the Wondjina painted themselves onto the rockface and their spirits descended into a sacred water-hole nearby, where their life-giving energy was available for all time.

In spite of their individual careers the fundamental unity of all these Wondjina primal beings is illustrated by the nature of the paintings. Although they range in size from a few feet to 16 feet (5 metres) they share common characteristics: they are painted against a white ground and the head of each is delineated by a strong band of red or yellow, creating a halo effect. The eyes and nose are linked and there is no mouth, for apparently if the Wondjina had a mouth it would rain incessantly. When the Wondjina are depicted as full length figures their bodies are usually painted with white stripes to represent falling rain.

Sir George Grey, the first European to see the Wondjina paintings in 1838, mistakenly thought they represented haloed priests wearing robes. Later European explorers

reckoned they were the work of oriental visitors of long ago.

An interesting observation of W. Arndt's is that massed heads of Wondjina resemble the banks of cumulo-nimbus clouds which herald the arrival of the rainy season. Backed by the sun or lightning each 'head' of the cloud seems to have a dark head-band and a surrounding halo of light.

The Wondjina are frequently to be found near paintings of the Rainbow Snake, known in this area as Galeru (Kaleru, Galaru), Ungud or Ungur. Indeed they are often identified as one and the same and certainly share the same concern with the regularity of the rain and the production of spirit children.

The paintings are still retouched occasionally at the end of the dry season to bring rains. In some galleries paintings of animals and plants were also retouched to bring about their increase. A dead person's bones were painted with red ochre and placed in the cave of his clan's Wondjina while his spirit descended into the nearby pool and returned to the Ungud to await reincarnation.

Designs and figures symbolising lightning, thunder and other storm phenomena are frequently to be found alongside the Wondjina. One gallery of Wondjina-like figures are called Garirinji and it was believed that if these were activated they had the power to unleash tornadoes.

The Lightning Brothers

For those who have seen the astonishing way a desert blossoms after rain, it is not surprising that of all the elemental forces of nature it is the rain that Aborigines most frequently associated with regeneration. Almost overnight, after the first rains have fallen in inland and northern Australia, the harsh ground is clothed with tender green. Before the rain the air is heavy and moisture-laden, the clouds bank up and the horizon is lit by distant lightning. But these signs do not always mean that relief is at hand. In this country the tension can build up over days, weeks, months, without rain actually falling, so it is again not surprising to find a proliferation of Dreamtime beings identified with rain-associated phenomena; the thunder, the lightning, the rainbow, the rainclouds and the rain itself, as well as frogs that appear when the pools are full of water again.

At an important rain-dreaming centre of the Wardaman at Delamere on the Daly River in the Northern Territory, much of the ritual was apparently focused on the Lightning Brothers whose images look down from the walls of a rock shelter. The important initiation rite of sub-incision was said to have been introduced by them. The two brothers fought over the charms of Cananda, wife of the elder brother Tcabuinji.

The younger brother Wagtjadbulla was killed, some say by his brother's boomerang, others say by his stone axe. In the painting the 12-foot (4-metre) figure of the young brother towers over the elder who carries a forked object beneath his left arm. One inquirer was told by his aboriginal informant that this was Cananda, but others claimed it was the axe used as the weapon and that Tcabuinji could split whole trees with it when he struck as lightning.

The axe certainly seems to be a symbol commonly associated with lightning, not only in Australia but

also in Europe and Southeast Asia. At Oenpelli in the Northern Territory drawings of the Lightning Man, Mamaragan, show him with stone axes on his joints. He lived at the bottom of a water-hole in the dry season and in the wet season he rode on the tops of the thunderclouds. His voice was the thunder and he struck down with his stone axes at the trees and the people. In eastern Australia similar characteristics were sometimes attributed to Dhurramulan, whose voice was the thunder. Some rock galleries show him in conjunction with weapons.

Other design motifs which the painting of the Lightning Brothers shares with those of rain-associated beings are their body stripes representing rain, and their lack of a mouth. Attached to their heads are two objects which are more like horns or antennae than ears. Some say that these make them like the gecko, the small lizard that can walk on overhanging surfaces, as the lightning does when it crosses the sky. Curiously enough the Rainbow Snake (the most important of all rain-associated beings), is sometimes described as having horns.

Above The dreamtime story of how Taipan, the snake man's son, stole blue-tongue lizard's wife and was speared, is re-enacted in totemic clan dances at Aurukun. The carved head represents Taipan. (Note similar headdress on p. 127 bottom.)

Opposite The row of flying foxes (fruit bats) painted on the rock face of the general camp shelter leading to an inner sacred cave in the Quinkan complex of caves, Cape York, may mark the border between the secular and the sacred. Interpretation remains uncertain because the people who so vividly depicted the bush life around them were brutally and rapidly wiped out in the 1870s at the time of the Palmer River gold rush.

The Rainbow Snake

The iridescence of pearl shell, the glitter of quartz crystal, the phosphorescence of the sea at night, sunlight trapped in water droplets above a waterfall; these things are for Aborigines the signs and symbols of the Great Snake whose body arches across the sky as the rainbow. On earth he makes his home in the deep rock pools and water-holes which are the reservoirs of the life-giving rain he has sent down. As his tracks cross the continent his name changes: from the north-west and across into the Northern Territory he is known as Galeru, Ungur, Wonungur, Worombi, Wonambi, Wollunqua, Yurlunggur, Julunggul and Langal; in Queensland his names include Yero and Taipan and in the south-east he is Mindi and Karia, and so on.

In the Dreamtime the Rainbow Snake co-existed with the other totemic ancestors; he shared with them the shaping of the landscape, particularly the great waterways, and he produced spirit children. Yet he

stands out above the rest because of his particular concern with the regeneration of nature and human fertility. In the Mother cults of Arnhem Land the Great Snake is sometimes identified with the mother herself, sometimes with her male companion, sometimes with both. In many places 'his' sex is not clear and in Australia as in other parts of the world the snake symbolises the ambisexuality of the creator.

There is also a creation-destruction or good-evil polarity about the concept of the Rainbow Snake. His power is so awe-inspiring that it must not be meddled with. Pregnant and menstruating women must take particular care not to defile his pools and in the north-east young men who have been recently sub-incised fear to drink from the river in case Kaleru seizes them. This association between the Rainbow Snake and blood is a strong theme in the Wikmunkan myth about Taipan, as it was told to U. McConnel.

Taipan's son stole the wife of the blue-tongued lizard. The angry

husband caught the pair and killed the boy. He tore his heart out and gave it to the father. Taipan made a gift of the blood to man and as a consequence he controls the physiological processes of men; the circulation of the blood and women's menstrual flow. Taipan was considered to be a great healer and sorcerer. His anger was roused particularly by the breaking of the rules which govern relationships between the sexes. If incest was committed or a woman withheld her promised daughter Taipan threw his blood-red knife, which he held by a long string. When he threw the knife, the thunder roared and the lightning flashed.

Disease as well as flood is an expression of the Great Snake's wrath. When smallpox was introduced by the Europeans the Aborigines near Melbourne called it the scale of Mindi. In the late 1840s there was considerable excitement among the Aborigines because it was believed that Mindi was coming and not even friendly settlers would be

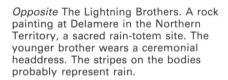

spared the horrors of Mindi's plague.

Rainmakers and medicine men can tap the destructive and the healing powers of the Great Snake by manipulating objects like quartz crystal and pearl shell from which emanate his power. In the north-west the medicine man's initiation into this art involved a journey to the sky on the back of the Rainbow Snake. Only medicine men would dare to venture into a pool sacred to the Rainbow Snake.

This fear of the Rainbow Snake gives rise to an element of propitiation in the Aborigine's approach to him. In the initiation ceremonies of eastern Arnhem Land it is said that Julunggul swallows the young boys. The implication of this is that by letting her do so the rest of the camp is saved from destruction. But even in this role the duality of Julunggul's character is made very clear because the great snake later vomits up the young boys — a symbolic rebirth that marks their transition from childhood to manhood.

Kunmanggur the Rainbow Snake and Tjinimin the Bat

In a myth told by the Murinbata of the north-west of the Northern Territory to W. Stanner, Kunmanggur the Rainbow Snake was cast as a powerful father figure whose authority and sexual supremacy was challenged by Tjinimin the Bat. The women he controlled were described as his daughters the green parrot women. One day the two girls sought their father's permission to go in search of food. No sooner had they left the camp than their brother who lusted after them also left on the pretext that he was going to visit his relatives, the flying fox-people. Instead he followed his sisters and forced his attentions on them, using them cruelly. The following day the girls determined to have their revenge. They crossed the river bed ahead of him and then, turning, they 'sang' the hornets to come and sting him and the tide to sweep over him. Tjinimin was carried away but after a while he struggled out on to dry land. Seeing the girls' fire at the top

of a cliff he again approached them. They agreed to throw down a rope to pull him up. He began to climb and just as he reached the top they cut the rope. He fell to the rocks below, breaking all his bones. But that was not the end of Tjinimin. His own magic songs restored his bones and he tested his power by cutting off his nose and restoring it again.

Assured of his power he next planned the murder of his father. For his part Kunmanggur must have been aware of Tjinimin's infamous conduct because the green parrot women had returned to the camp, but it is not explicitly mentioned and the plot continues to unfold with primal inevitablity.

Tjinimin's deception continued; he made a spear which he pretended belonged to his father. When he returned to camp he kept it hidden. On the way he invited all the people to a big ceremony and fired the hill-tops to announce its commencement. The famous songman, the Diver Bird, came and Kunmanggur played the drone pipe while Tjinimin led the

dancing. He danced so as to arouse
the women's desire and then, at the
peak of his performance, he drew
forth the spear and slew his father.
Instantly all the dancers were transformed into flying foxes and birds
and flew away crying with grief.
Tjinimin fled – none dared to stop
him.

The old man went from place to
place seeking ways to staunch his
blood and heal the wound. Wherever
he rested life-giving water welled up.
In one place he left the shape of his
body and his footprints on the rock
wall, in others he left his possessions;
his stone axe, fishing net and forehead
band. At last he came to the sea, and
entering it he gathered the fire of the
world and placed it on his head as a
headdress. Slowly it dawned on the
watchers that he intended to go
down, carrying the fire with him. Too
late the last brand was snatched
away; it had already gone out. Then
Pilirin the Kestrel gave fire back to
men by using two firesticks. This had
never been done before.

This powerful vision of the
founding drama as a primal tragedy is
a compelling comment on the human
condition as it appears to the Murinbata. W. Stanner, to whom this myth
was told, defines the underlying
theme as one of 'perennial goodness
with suffering'. Furthermore he found
that the more details he sought about
Kunmanggur the more this powerful
image conjured up by the myth
receded into ambiguity. Sometimes
Kunmanggur the Rainbow Snake
appeared to be either bi-sexual, or a
woman; even when he was described

as male he had the breasts of a woman. There is also obvious phallic symbolism in the belief that the rainbow was formed by the water he spat from his drone pipe and that this water also carried the spirit children and the young flying foxes he made.

Elsewhere in Arnhem Land the theme of the Rainbow Snake was frequently an important element in the myth which validated the ritual of the fertility cult. Amongst the Murinbata themselves it was unaccompanied by a rite, their most important revelationary ritual being sanctioned by the myth of Kalwadi, the Old Woman. Stanner suggests that there may be an historical explanation for this shift in emphasis from the father figure to the 'Mother of us All', for it parallels an apparently recent change in the system of social organisation from a patrilineal to a matrilineal emphasis.

The Great Mother

Along the coastal fringe of the Northern Territory the sub-tropical growth and the plentiful supply of fish, dugong, turtle and crocodile, as well as the great variety of wild fowl and small game make nature appear more generous than she seems in many other parts of the continent. Yet the rhythm of life in this tropical region is bound to the endless cycle of dry and wet seasons which regulates the abundance of the food resources, and in turn inspires the deep concern with fertility that dominates the religious cults of the area.

In the days before European settlement, the north-west monsoons which bring the wet season also brought contacts with the outside world. The Malays and Macassans came down in their praus to trade and fish and returned with the southeast winds laden with trepang and pearl shell. Before them had come the legendary golden-skinned Baijini who may have been sea gipsies of the Malay archipelago, and who were sometimes described by the Aborigines as the contemporaries of their

Right A great cycle of ceremonies performed at Milingimbi, Arnhem Land, involves the re-enactment of episodes in the myth of the Wawilak sisters and their children who were swallowed by the Great Snake, here represented by a ground drawing.

Opposite An exceptionally fine bark painting by the artist Mawalan of Yirrkalla in Eastern Arnhem Land illustrates the Djankawa myth of the dhuwa moiety; annotated by R. M. Berndt. In the top right-hand panel the artist has drawn himself, seated, in front of his goanna-tailed rangga, singing songs from the Djankawa cycle. The Djankawa sisters giving birth to the first Aborigines is realisticaly illustrated in the section second from the top, and the same theme is represented semi-abstractly in the bottom section. In the left-hand side of the panel above it are the special tree rangga used to make the first trees. Alongside are the Djankawa, two sisters and a brother, and two symbols of the sun, one at sunset and the other at sunrise. The Djankawa have an affinity with the sun. Art Gallery of New South Wales, Sydney.

own ancestral beings who were also said to have come from across the sea.

In western Arnhem Land the Mother-Who-Made-Us-All, called by some tribes Waramurungundju and others Imberombera, came out of the sea from the direction of Indonesia. She made the landscape and from her body she produced many children, animals and plants which she distributed. She assigned a language to each group of people. On the other side of Arnhem Land, R. M. Berndt recorded the songs the Alawa people sing of the coming of the Great Mother, Kunapipi, to the mouth of the Roper River:

*Tidal water flowing, white foam on
    the waves.
Fresh water from the rains flows into
    the river.
There are the paperback trees: their
    soft bark falls into the water . . .
Rain falls from the clouds . . .
Waters of the river are swirling . . .
She, Kunapipi, emerges, and walks
    on dry land.*

The Djankawu

North of Roper River, also on the eastern coast, Laindjung rose out of the sea, at Blue Mud Bay, his face foam-stained and his body patterned with salt water marks. These patterns and the accompanying ritual he gave to the Yirritja moiety.

For in this north-east corner of Arnhem Land the Wulamba people classify everything in the universe as belonging to the dhuwa or the Yirritja moiety.

This division was laid down in the *wongar* or Dreamtime by the Djankawu beings, two sisters and a brother who crossed the sea from Bralgu in the east and landed where Port Bradshaw is now. Each moiety owns its own myths and ritual and is responsible for initiating the ceremonies and acting the principle roles, but members of both moieties participate in the cult activities so that the arrangement is a way of sharing ceremonial responsibilities rather than representing a division. Of the two myth complexes those that relate

to the Djankawu creative beings are certainly the most important. Their journey is celebrated in a great cycle of some 500 songs rich in cryptic and symbolic imagery to which the translations and annotations of R. M. Berndt in *Djanggawul* provide a useful key.

The eternally pregnant Djankawu (Djanggawul, Djanggau, Djunkgao) sisters are a dual manifestation of the Fertility Mother. The cycle begins with an evocative description of the two women, their brother and a companion, Bralbral, paddling along, following the path of the morning star which guides them in their journey from Bralgu, the dhuwa island home of the dead. (The Wulamba believe that the morning star is really a ball of seagull feathers attached to a long string which is played out by the spirits.) With them they carry the conical plaited ngainmara mat, the sacred dilly bag and the rangga emblems to use in their sacred ritual.

The words of the first song recreate the scene:

I, Djanggawul, look back; and see the rays of light leading back to our island of Bralgu
Shine that falls on the paddle as it's dipped into and drawn from the sea:
Shine that spreads from the Star's rays, from Bralgu.
The Morning Star skimming the sea's surface, sent by the dancing spirits there,
Shine following us from Bralgu, like a feathered ball with string attached.
Foam and bubbles rise to the sea's surface: a large wave carries us on its crest.
The roar of the sea, the sound of our paddling, the spray of the waves, its salty smell!
We carry with us the sacred mat within which lie the sacred rangga objects.

In both the songs and the ritual the mat represents the womb; the rangga are sometimes phallic symbols and sometimes identified with the children the sisters produce. In some versions, the sisters are themselves identified with the sun.

As the sun came up and warmed their backs they likened its rays to the red parakeet-feathered string with which they decorated the rangga. After they arrived at the Place of the Sun, the present Port Bradshaw, the party began to walk overland. Wherever Djankawu thrust his walking stick-rangga into the ground, water welled up. The same thing happened when the sisters thrust their yam stick-ranggas into the ground, and when they used the tree-rangga trees sprang up. But their most important activity was the removal of the children from the mat and the dilly bag and from the sisters' wombs, for they were constantly being made pregnant by their brother.

They left animals and plants for the people they made and they also left them sacred rangga emblems and taught them the *nara* ceremonies. They not only met other ancestral beings but also the Baijini whom they forced to move.

The women played the principal part in all these activities until one day they left their sacred objects in the main camp while they went to gather shellfish. The brother and his companions returned to camp and stole the sacred paraphernalia. The whistle of a mangrove bird warned the sisters that something was wrong and fearing a fire had burnt their possessions they hurried back. They discovered the men's tracks and followed them but as they drew near the men the latter began to beat the sticks and chant the sacred songs. The women drew back afraid. The power to perform the sacred ritual had passed from them to the men, who have retained it. In *Djanggawul*, in the 140th song, the sisters sing:

Let us kneel down in the mud, crawling along!
We leave it for them, for our younger Brother.
We shall grind the cycad nut, preparing the bread for them, for our Brother!
We shall whiten our hands with flour, for it is better that way ...
With our hands we shall hold the grinding stone; we shall hang from our foreheads our bags of 'coffee' tree fibre, collecting foods ...
We leave that ritual for them for they want it that way.

As the Djankawu journeyed along the northern Arnhem Land coast towards the setting sun they continued their procreative activities and established the rules by which the people they made should live.

The idea that the women controlled the religious life until the sacred paraphernalia was stolen by the men or handed over to them, is a recurring theme in Aboriginal myths.

In the *nara* ceremonies in which the Djankawu story is re-lived the bough shade or hut on the sacred ground represents both the ngainmara mat and the womb of the mother. The ritual is revelationary in intent, designed to lead the fully initiated man deeper into the sacred life. But the women and the uninitiated are also involved, for in the ngainmara ceremony which is performed in the main camp, they are gathered together and hidden underneath mats. As the men dance round them poking at them with sticks and spears they wriggle in response like children in the womb. The climax comes with their emergence from under the mat re-living in their actions the primal birth of their ancestors from the wombs of Djankawu.

The Wawilak Sisters

The Wawilak (Wawalag, Wauwalak) sisters whose story is told in northeastern Arnhem Land are sometimes described as the daughters of the elder Djankawu sister, but although their myth substantiates the fertility cult of the area and they are concerned with fertility they are not creators. The important incident in their story is the encounter with the Great Python or Rainbow Snake Yurlunggur, or Julunggul.

In the Milingimbi version of the story as told to L. Warner, the sisters were said to have come from the south after having had incestuous relations with their clansmen. One of them was carrying a baby boy. As they travelled they named the animals and plants and spoke different languages in each territory they passed through. After a while the younger sister gave birth to a girl. They continued on towards the sea until unwittingly they camped beside Yurlunggur's water-hole. They prepared their food but as soon as they placed each animal and plant on the fire it jumped out and dived into the water-hole because it had taken on the sacredness of the well. Then the elder sister went to fetch water and profaned the pool with her menstrual blood. The great snake rose up in anger and the water spilled from the well and flooded the countryside – the rain fell. At last the women realised their danger and tried to stop the rain and the advance of the great snake towards them by singing and dancing. Whenever they paused he moved forward. At last they fell asleep and he swallowed them.

Above The inverted figure and distorted limbs of a sorcery painting, Mushroom rock, Cape York.

Top A painting on bark of a funeral ceremony by the artist Bunia, of Groote Eylandt. (*Top left*) A man lies dying on a funeral platform. (*Bottom left*) The didjeridu player and the dancers perform until he dies. (*Top right*) The spirit man and his two wives also dance and play until he dies. After death the man's spirit leaves the platform and begins the long journey to the spirit world, crossing over the great snake. (*Bottom right*) He kills a fish with a stone for food for the journey.

Again he raised himself to the sky and all the other great pythons of the other centres also raised themselves up. The great snakes talked together about the ritual they shared although they spoke different languages. Then they told each other what they had just eaten. When it came to Yurlung-gur's turn he was ashamed and at first refused to say, but at last he admitted to having eaten the two sisters and their children. Then he fell down, splitting the ground, and spewed up the women and children. Green ants

bit them and revived them. Again he swallowed them and again he regurgi-tated them, and each time he rose up and fell down he made a ceremonial ground for each of the great rituals with which this myth is associated. The most important of these ceremonies are the Djungawon or Djungguan, the Kunapipi or Guna-bibi, and the Ngurlmak, or Ulmark. All of them are both initiatory and revelationary in intent, although the Djunggawon is concerned particu-larly with circumcision. In each the central theme of the myth, namely the swallowing and regurgitation of the sisters by the snake is ritually represented. In the Kunapipi the ceremonial ground stands for the body of the great snake and a hole is dug to represent the sacred well.

In some variants of the myth the great python is said to be the women's brother. In others it is female, Julunggul for example, and is therefore more easily identified with the image of the swallowing-regurgi-tating mother of the ritual and of other myths. In the Djunggawon the great snake is represented by the trumpet Yurlunggur (Julunggul). This is an alternative name for Kunapipi, the Great Mother, and it is also one of the names given to the Lightning Snake. In the Ngurlmak the same great snake is called Uwar, represented by a hollow log drum.

One can take any one of these names and establish links with other myths and rites throughout the whole northern section of the Northern Territory, thus demonstrating not only the dynamic nature of the cults of the area but also the common concern with fertility which flows through them and finds expression in the interlocking images of the Great Mother and the Rainbow Snake.

Yirawadbad the Snake Man

In Western Arnhem Land Urbar is the name of a cult, and the beating of the urbar drum summons the men to the ceremonial ground. A low whistling sound introduces the first dancers and this is said to be the wind whistling through the horns of the Rainbow Snake as he raises his body up and across the sky to announce the coming of the wet season.

Yirawadbad was angry with a mother and daughter because the daughter who was betrothed to him refused to sleep with him. He made a hollow drum and hid inside it in snake form. The women came in search of small game and peered into the log. When the daughter looked the snake shut his eyes and she saw only darkness, when the mother looked he opened his eyes and as she saw right through she thought it was empty. The women placed their hands in the log and were bitten and died.

Kunapipi – Kalwadi – Kadjari Constellation

Because the Wawilak sisters came from the south they are sometimes identified with the Mungamunga girls, who in the south of Arnhem Land are described as the daughters of Kunapipi. This is the Kunapipi who lends her name to the Kunapipi-Kalwadi-Kadjari complex of ceremonies which are perhaps the most

widespread of the cults of the Great Mother. In recent years it has extended west from the Roper River in a wide sweep that encompasses almost all Arnhem Land and continues across the central-west of the Northern Territory into Western Australia.

In the myth told by the Mara of the Roper River area to R. M. Berndt, Kunapipi exploited the charms of her daughters to ensnare young men whom she killed and ate. When she tried to vomit them up only the bones appeared and the ants weren't able to revive them. This state of affairs continued for some time until a very powerful man, Eaglehawk, decided to investigate the disappearance of so many men. He caught Kunapipi in the act and killed her. As she died she cried out, and her sound entered every tree. Eaglehawk cut the tree, and it gave back her cry.

In the Murinbata myth of the Old Woman, Kalwadi, as told to W. Stanner, the rebirth of the children was made possible by her death. Mutjingga, for that was her name, was left in charge of the children. She tended them carefully and when the time came for them to rest she made a sleeping place in the shade. She pretended to look for lice in one child's hair and swallowed her whole. Then she swallowed another nine children and left the camp. On their return, the parents were horrified to

find their children missing and searched for the guardian-grand-mother. Splitting into two parties they followed the river on opposite banks. At first the water was clear but then it became murky and they knew they were coming closer to her, so they hurried ahead and then turned back to face her. As they saw her big eyes appear above the surface, Left Hand pierced her legs with his spear and Right Hand broke her neck with his club. To her cries of protest they replied: 'Yours was the fault.' For they truly regretted killing her. They cut her open and removed the children alive from her womb, because this was where they had gone when she swallowed them. They washed, painted, and adorned them and returned them to their mothers who cried out: 'She swallowed you.'

This too is a tragic theme. It is the validating myth of the highest revelationary ceremony of the Murinbata called the Punj. The young neophytes approach this with fear and awe because they believe they are about to be swallowed and vomited up by the Old Woman. They emerge from the sacred ground to a new adult role in the society.

Why Men Die

Aborigines believe that after death at least some part of a person's spiritual

essence is re-united with the Eternal Dreaming. Sometimes this implies a return to the site laid down by the totemic ancestor but over most of eastern Australia the spirit rejoined the heroes in the sky world. The people of the lower Murray River district believed that Ngurunderi established the route the soul should take when he journeyed to Kangaroo Island off the South Australian coast and then went up into the sky. Two ideas which are found elsewhere in Oceania also occurred along the east coast. They are the belief in the existence of a Leaping Place for souls and the belief that the land of the dead was reached by crossing a hazardous log or tree bridge. In parts of the north-west it was thought that the land of the dead lay over the sea to the west. In north-eastern Arnhem Land dhuwa spirits are ferried to the island of Bralgu by Nganug the paddlemaker, while Yirritja spirits journey to Badu, an island somewhere in the Torres Straits. There they are welcomed by the Kultana, or Guldana, whose duty it is to light fires to guide them to their destination.

In spite of these beliefs death is still regarded as a crisis and few deaths are thought to be from natural causes. An inquest is held and retribution sought. A part of a man's spirit may also linger round his old haunts and cause trouble.

The Aranda affirmed that a primal murder was the explanation of the origin of death. When the curlews emerged in the Dreamtime the women came out first, followed by the men. The first man was thought to have followed too closely behind the women so the others killed him by pointing a magic bone at him. After they buried him the women began to dance round the grave and slowly he broke through the crust again. Seeing this the magpie flew down and speared him, then trampled him back into the ground again. The grief-stricken women flew away as curlews and mankind lost the chance of becoming immortal. Throughout Australia curlews are associated with death and mourning, no doubt because of their mournful cry.

The Wonguri-Mandjigai song cycle of the Moon-bone from Arnhem Bay, translated by R. M. Berndt, tells how Moon, a man, lived with his sister, Dugong, by the side of the claypan which, in the rainy season, becomes a billabong. Dugong complained that the place was dangerous because the leeches bit her as she searched for edible roots. So one day she went into the sea and turned into a dugong. 'When I die,' she said, 'I won't come back, but you may pick up my bones.'

Moon replied that he didn't want to die, that he would go into the sky. When he grew old he went down into the sea and threw his bones away, to be washed up as the nautilus shell. After three days he reappeared and gradually regained his size and strength by eating lotus and lily roots.

Now the New Moon is hanging, having cast away his bone:

Gradually he grows larger, taking on new bone and flesh.
Over there, far away, he has shed his bone: he shines on the place of the Lotus Root, and the place of the Dugong,
On the place of the Evening Star, of the Dugong's Tail, of the moonlit Claypan...
Gradually growing, his new bone growing as well.
Over there, the horns of the old reeding moon bent down, sank into the place of the Dugong:
His horns were pointing towards the place of the Dugong....
Now the New Moon swells to fullness, his bone grown larger.
He looks on the water, hanging above it, at the place of the Lotus.
There he comes into sight, hanging above the sea, growing larger and older...
There far away he has come back, hanging over the clans near Milingimbi...
Hanging there in the sky above those clans...

More power to the voice of a people who can express their beliefs with such poetry and rich imagination. In spite of the pressures of modern technicalogical society which are being brought to bear on the Aborigines, their special bond with their land is proving resilient. Nor can we afford to reject the legacy of the timeless ideas expressed in their myths.

Further Reading List

Some of the most important sources consulted are listed below.

GENERAL

Alkire, W. H. *Coral Islanders*. AHM Publishing Corporation, 1978.

Bellwood, P. *Man's Conquest of the Pacific*. Collins, London, 1978.

Dixon, R. B. *Mythology of Oceania (The Mythology of all Races,* Vol. 9). Cooper Square Pubs. Inc., New York, 1922.

Guiart, J. *The Arts of the South Pacific*. Thames & Hudson, London, 1963.

White, J. P. and O'Connell, J. F. *A Prehistory of Australia, New Guinea and Sohul*. Academic Press, New York, 1982.

POLYNESIA

Beckwith, M. *Hawaiian Mythology*. Yale University Press, 1940.

Gifford, E. W. *Tongan Myths and Tales*. Bulletin 8, Bernice P. Bishop Museum, Honolulu, 1924.

Grey, Sir George. *Polynesian Mythology*. Whitcombe & Tombs, Ltd., London and Christchurch, 1965.

Handy, E. S. C. *Marquesan Legends*. Bulletin 69, Bernice P. Bishop Museum, Honolulu, 1930.
Polynesian Religion. Bulletin 34, Bernice P. Bishop Museum, Honolulu, 1927.

Henry, T. *Ancient Tahiti*. Bulletin 48, Bernice P. Bishop Museum, Honolulu, 1928.

Kirtley, B. F. *A Motif-Index of Traditional Polynesian Narratives*. University of Hawaii Press, Honolulu, 1971.

Luomola, K. *Voices on the Wind*. Bernice P. Bishop Museum Press, Honolulu, 1955.
Maui-of-a-thousand tricks. Bulletin 198, Bernice P. Bishop Museum, 1949.

Métraux, A. *Easter Island*. André Deutsch, London, 1957.

Simmons, D. R. *The Great New Zealand Myth*. Reed, Wellington, Sydney, London, 1976.

Suggs, R. C. *Island Civilisations of Polynesia*. Mentor Books, London, 1960.

MICRONESIA

Burrows, E. G. *A Flower in my Ear*. University of Washington Press, Seattle, 1963.

Grimble, Sir Arthur. *A Pattern of Islands*. John Murray, Ltd., London, 1952.

Lessa, W. A. *Tales from Ulithi Atoll*. Folklore Studies 13, University of California Press, 1961.

MELANESIA

Burridge, K. O. L. *Mambu*. Methuen & Co. Ltd., London, 1960.

Codrington, R. *The Melanesians. Studies in their History, Anthropology, and Folklore*. Clarendon Press, Oxford, 1891.

Drabbe, P. *Folktales from Netherlands New Guinea*. University of Sydney (*Oceania,* vols 18, 19, 20), 1947–50.

Humphreys, C. B. *The Southern New Hebrides*. Cambridge University Press, 1926.

Landtman, G. *Folktales of the Kiwai Papuans*. Finnish Society of Literature, Helsinki, 1917.

Mead, Margaret, *The Mountain Arapesh*. American Natural History Museum, Papers 36, 37, 40 & 41. 1938–49.

Powdermaker, H. *Life in Lesu*. Williams & Norgate, London, 1933.

Wheeler, G. C. *Mono Alu Folklore*. Routledge, Kegan Paul, Ltd., London, 1926.

AUSTRALIA

Berndt, C. H. & R. M. *The World of the First Australians*. Angus & Robertson, Sydney, 1965.

Berndt, R. M. (Ed.) *Australian Aboriginal Art*. Ure Smith Pty., Ltd., Sydney, The Macmillan Company, New York, and Collier-Macmillan Ltd., London and Toronto, 1964.

Hiatt, L. R. (Ed.) *Australian Aboriginal Mythology (Australian Aboriginal Studies* No. 50). Australian Institute of Aboriginal Studies, Canberra, 1975.

Howard, M. C. (Ed.) *'Whitefella Business'*. Institute for the Study of Human Issues, Philadelphia, 1978.

Howitt, A. H. *The Native Tribes of South-eastern Australia*. Macmillan & Co. Ltd., London, 1904.

McConnel, Ursula. *Myths of the Munkan*. Cambridge University Press, 1957.

Stanner, W. E. H. *On Aboriginal Religion*. University of Sydney (*Oceania* Monograph 11) 1963.

Strehlow, T. G. H. *Aranda Traditions*. Melbourne University Press, 1947.

Acknowledgements

The author is deeply grateful to the staff of the Museum of Mankind Library for the skilled assistance afforded to her over many years. The author and the publishers acknowledge the following for permission to quote from existing works. Bishop Museum Press, Honolulu: 'The Song of Hiro', p. 37, from Bulletin 48 *Ancient Tahiti*, T. Henry; the Tongan *solo*, p. 50, from Bulletin 8 *Tongan Myths and Tales*, E. W. Gifford; Maui's chant, p. 58, chants in Rata's story, p. 65, 67, all from Bulletin 148 *Tuamotuan Legends* trans. by J. F. Stimson. John Murray Ltd.: Nareau's verses, p. 72, trans. by Sir Arthur Grimble in *A Pattern of Islands*. Whitcombe & Tombs, Ltd.: extract from Introduction to Sir George Grey's *Polynesian Mythology*, p. 19; Maui, p. 60, and the creation, p. 31, 33. Constable & Co. Ltd.: Hawaiian prayer, p. 24, trans. by W. V. Westervelt in *Legends, Gods and Ghosts*. Bureau of American Ethnology, Smithsonian Institution: *hula* song of Pele, p. 44, and Hi'iaki's rain song, p. 45, trans. by N. B. Emerson in Bulletin 38 *Unwritten Literature of Hawaii*. Melbourne University Press: Nyungu's song, p. 121, trans. by Ursula McConnel in *Myths of the Munkan*. Professor E. M. Berndt: trans. of Alawa song of Kunapipi, p. 137, in *Kunapipi*, and Song

140 from the Djanggawul Cycle, p. 138, in *The Djanggawul*. Professor Berndt and the editors of *Mankind*: trans. of song 1 of the cycle, p. 138, in Vol. 4, No. 6. Professor Berndt and the editor of *Oceania*: trans. of song 12 of Wonguri-Mandjigai Song Cycle of the Moon-Bone, p. 141, in Vol. 19, No. 1.

Photographs David Attenborough 133; Dr. P. H. Beighton 43; Bernice P. Bishop Museum, Honolulu 47; British Museum, London 25, 26, 29 top, 29 bottom, 37 left, 53, 56, 57, 73, 74, 75, 99, 112 bottom; Bruce Coleman – Nicholas Devore 10; G. Donkin 122, 132; Kerry Dundas 96, 97, 136; Field Museum of Natural History, Chicago, Illinois 86, 105 left; Frobenius Institut, Frankfurt 128; Glasgow Museums and Art Galleries 35, 37 right; Karel Kupka 135; Linden-Museum, Stuttgart 94, 95; K. Lommel, Munich 124, 125; Metropolitan Museum of Art, New York 32 left, 112 top; Musée de l'Homme, Paris 49, 81, 93; Museum für Völkerkunde, Basel 106; Museum für Völkerkunde, Hamburg 55, 109 right; Museum für Völkerkunde, Vienna 44; National Gallery of South Australia, Adelaide 129; National Library of Australia, Canberra 92, 100–101; National Maritime Museum, London 13 bottom, 18–19; Newnes Books 29 bottom, 39, 46,

62, 70, 72, 78, 85, 87, 91, 99, 103, 103, 111; Peabody Museum of Archaeology and Ethnology, Harvard University, Cambridge, Massachusetts 59; W. H. Pedersen, Canberra 134; Pitt Rivers Museum, Oxford half title, 8 top, 61, 67, 84 bottom, 104; Axel Poignant, London frontispiece 6–7, 8 bottom, 9, 11, 12, 15, 16, 17 top, 17 bottom, 19 top, 19 bottom, 22–23, 27, 28, 30, 31, 32 right, 34, 36, 38 right, 42, 48, 50, 51, 52, 58, 60, 63, 65, 66, 83, 84 top, 88, 89, 98, 100, 107, 108 left, 109 left, 114–115, 116, 117, 118, 119, 120, 121, 123, 124, 126–127, 127 top, 127 bottom, 130, 130–131, 137, 139 top, 139 bottom, 140, 141; Harvey W. Reed, Honolulu 14, 71, 79; Royal Anthropological Institute of Great Britain and Ireland, London 110; University Museum, Philadelphia, Pennsylvania 13 top, 38 left, 77; University Museum of Archaeology and Ethnology, Cambridge 24, 45, 64, 90, 105 right, 108 right, 113 left, 113 right.
The photographs on pages 68 to 69 and that on page 80 are from *East is a bird* by Thomas Gladwin, Harvard University Press, 1970, the former taken by Peter Silverman and the latter by Thomas Gladwin.

INDEX